Word Among us

About the authors

MARTIN KITCHEN is a graduate in modern languages and theology of the University of London, and holds a doctorate in New Testament Studies from the University of Manchester. He prepared for ordination at King's College, London, and with the Southwark Ordination Course, and is a Residentiary Canon of Durham Cathedral.

GEORGIANA HESKINS teaches Religious Studies at Eltham College, an independent school for boys in south-east London. She is a priest-vicar at Southwark Cathedral and lives in the Borough of Greenwich, within sight of the Thames Barrier and the Millennium Dome. She has also served as Tutor at the South East Institute for Theological Education where she taught Pastoral and Biblical Studies. Her own preparation for ordination was at King's College, London, and at Westcott House in Cambridge, and most of her preaching experience has been gained in London.

STEPHEN MOTYER spent some years at the pulpit face trying to make the lectionary live in rural Hertfordshire, before taking up his present post as New Testament Lecturer at London Bible College. Before that he taught at Oak Hill College, and looks back with thankfulness on theological studies at Cambridge, Bristol, Tübingen and London. With the other authors of this Commentary, he shares a vision for inspiring preaching at the heart of worship.

Word Among Us

*Insights into the Scripture readings
for Sundays and major Holy Days*

Year A

Martin Kitchen, Georgiana Heskins
and Stephen Motyer

CANTERBURY
PRESS

Norwich

© Martin Kitchen, Georgiana Heskins and Stephen Motyer,
2001

First published 2001 by The Canterbury Press Norwich
(a publishing imprint of Hymns Ancient & Modern Limited,
a registered charity)
St Mary's Works, St Mary's Plain,
Norwich, Norfolk, NR3 3BH

British Library Cataloguing in Publication Data

A catalogue record for this book is available
from the British Library

ISBN 1-85311-414-6

Typeset by Rowland Phototypesetting Limited,
Bury St Edmunds, Suffolk
Printed in Great Britain by
Biddles Limited, Guildford and King's Lynn

Contents

Preface

A banner which hangs in Durham Cathedral commemorates the members of the Haswell Lodge of the Durham Miners Association. Its motto reads, 'They being dead yet speaketh', and the singular verb jars happily with the plural pronoun. It seems to demand a reading that suggests that what these self-sacrificing miners speak, many though they are, is one. There is a sense – though it must not be pressed – in which the scriptures, for all their diversity, may be read in the same way, for they speak of God, who is one, according to Jewish, Christian and Muslim tradition.

However, the diversity and complexity of scripture must also be accorded their rightful place. The scriptures are testimony to a faith which is not monochrome; and the fact that three faiths can claim to be 'people of the Book' should alert us to the dangers of any facile assumption that those faiths 'are all the same really'. The same may be said of the scriptures themselves: they span centuries, their authors varied – and differed. Their message is complex, and whatever meaning may be found in them is dear-achieved. Faithful preachers, even those who make use of this book, will wrestle with the text of scripture every bit as much as have we who have had the pleasure of working together on producing it. There is no easy path to meaning, for straight is the gate and narrow is the way that leads to life, both in text and in eternity.

The Revised Common Lectionary is now well-established in the usage of the churches. The previous edition of this book, *Word of Promise*, met a very favourable response from the Bible-reading public, as did the former volume in this series, *Word in Our Time*, which had as its precursor, *Word of Life*. All this suggests that the desire for assistance in the reading of scripture is real, and that what we have written is proving of help to some.

It has been a pleasure to work again with Georgiana Heskins and

Stephen Motyer. It has already been said that we represent slightly different theological traditions within Anglicanism, yet we have in common the desire to see that God's people are equipped to read the Bible with understanding. That way they may gain some help in applying its message to the daily calling and task of Christian discipleship.

It is a further pleasure to include again Michael Hampel's contribution to this volume in the form of his essay on the seasons of the liturgical year. Michael is Precentor of Durham Cathedral, and his enthusiasm for and knowledge of liturgical tradition is equalled by his daily competence in leading and singing the services here.

Christine Smith and Anna Hardman have proved patient and wise counsellors, and our families and colleagues have been characteristically generous in their support and encouragement of our work.

MARTIN KITCHEN
Durham Cathedral
Passiontide 2001

Introduction

On Reading St Matthew's Gospel

The first volume in this series of commentaries was entitled *Word in Our Time*. It took this title largely from an understanding of the written Gospel which forms the mainstay of the Lectionary in Year C, that of St Luke. The present volume bears the name *Word Among Us*, and this is derived from St Matthew's account of Jesus. For most of Christian history Matthew was believed to be the first of the Gospels to be written, and it was not until the rise of historical critical scholarship that this view – most clearly set out by St Augustine – was challenged.

But challenged it was, and successfully, so that it may now be said with a fair degree of confidence that the two Gospels of Matthew and Luke are dependent upon Mark. The three together are known as 'Synoptic', because it is possible to put all three in parallel columns in a synopsis. Matthew and Luke have in common (a) that they made use of Mark, (b) that they made use also of a sayings source, known as 'Q', and (c) that they both bear separate units of tradition which are peculiar to themselves. These units are known as 'M' and 'L' respectively. These statements inevitably over-simplify a complex set of research and arguments, but they represent the basis of Gospel research as it is currently understood and taught.

We have St Matthew to thank for a large amount of the teaching which is attributed to Jesus. This is presented, in the Gospel, in five separate blocks, the most well known of which is perhaps 'The Sermon on the Mount', in Matthew 5, the most popular form of the Lord's Prayer and much about the Church, including the controversial status of St Peter (and his successors) within it. The 'Great Commission' ('Go into all the world and preach the gospel to every creature . . .') is also found in this Gospel. There is no Ascension story in Matthew, for all that the Great Commission reads like an Ascension story; there is nothing of the continuing life of the Church in the world, in spite of its emphasis on the life of Jesus within the community – perhaps because Jesus does not disappear at the end, but promises to remain with his disciples, and the community's continuing life is given expression in the narrative as it progresses.

Luke has many of the more popular stories, and this may leave the reader a little puzzled as to why they are not in Matthew; even though he has stories of the nativity, these are different from Luke's. The answer lies partly in the availability of sources and partly in a difference of theological accent.

There is an emphasis on the Christian community in Matthew which is lacking in both Mark and Luke. Recent studies have suggested that the particular community for which Matthew was written was under threat, having recently separated from a Jewish synagogue. It therefore found itself in inevitable argument and conflict with Judaism; in this may be seen parallels to the fourth Gospel, though the opposition between church and synagogue is more stylized there. Charges of 'anti-semitism' against the New Testament authors have to reckon with the historical realities of the early Church's experience, which found itself under threat from the older and more established faith. What is clear is that the position in which the infant community found itself left it free to accept the validity of the conversion of Gentiles to faith in the risen Jesus, and the early ambivalence to this possibility is evidenced in its pages.

No doubt because of the link with Judaism, there is much in the Gospel about the fulfilment of prophecy. It is this fact that led us to the title, Word Among Us. Here the story of Jesus is seen against the background of the Word of God addressed to his ancient people of Israel and recorded in the Old Testament; there is a sense of fulfilment here which the other Gospels lack; their interests lie elsewhere. For Matthew, Jesus is not only the new Moses, the new Lawgiver, but also none other than Emanuel, 'With-Us-Is-God', and consequently the basis for a new understanding of the life of God within a human community.

One of the challenges to those who read this Gospel must be that of re-interpreting that sense of fulfilment and presence in a culture which, in any case, had a history which was not that of Israel; but more than that, which has to some extent lost much of its sense of the past. Such a statement is not to be read as a complaint; the

Church of Jesus Christ is always called to serve its contemporary setting. What must concern us, however, is how we make sense of a belief in one who fulfils the hopes of people, families and communities, when those very hopes and histories are unfocused. Perhaps, along with our reading and preaching of scripture, we need to be more perceptive in our listening.

The final volume in the series, a commentary on the readings for Year B, will follow next year and take its measure from the earliest of the Gospels, that of St Mark.

The Seasons of the Year –
a liturgical preface

The Christian year revolves around the great festivals of Easter and Christmas and developed from the celebration each Sunday of Christ's resurrection. From this fundamental liturgical routine, a more complex approach emerged as Christ's birth, death, resurrection and the sending of the Holy Spirit were commemorated throughout each calendar year. The Christian year thus provided stepping stones for pilgrims and patterns for worship which have informed all subsequent liturgical reform. The *Revised Common Lectionary* seeks to enhance the celebration of the Christian year and to convey its shape and cycle with greater clarity and breadth than hitherto. This is achieved particularly by dispensing with a thematic approach to the Sundays – while nevertheless relating lections to the themes of the major festivals – and by acknowledging some of the liturgical insights of recent years.

The beginning of the Christian year is established in its traditional position on the First Sunday of **Advent**. This season of preparation for the celebration of the birth of Christ is divided into a period of four Sundays, each of which looks towards his 'coming' or 'arrival'. This time-span has evolved from a longer six-Sunday period dating from fifth-century Gaul and possibly imitating the length of the Lenten period of preparation for Easter. Often overlooked is the two-fold nature of the advent of Christ: the season prepares for incarnation at Bethlehem but also for a second coming at the end of time. In this double context, the season's themes of death, judgement, heaven and hell make broader sense

As a season of preparation, Advent adopts the flavour of expectant self-examination; in the modern age, the urgency to prepare for Christmas in its commercial sense has caused Advent to lose much of its scope for spiritual preparation. An attempt has been made, therefore, to bring Advent forward by observing the **Kingdom** season which culminates in the festival of Christ the King on the Sunday next before Advent. Other November themes of All Saints, the departed and Remembrance are in keeping with a need to focus spiritually on Christ both as a fellow citizen in this world and as King in the world to come. The longer medieval period of preparation is thus restored. The 'pivotal' Kingdom season both prepares for Advent and concludes the previous year. The Christian year in effect becomes a seamless garment of commemoration and celebration.

Christmas is the great festival of the birth of Christ celebrating God's incarnation as human being in Bethlehem. It may have arisen out of the pagan celebration of the winter solstice on 25 December in the West and 6 January in the East; or its date may have been calculated on the basis of the date of the death of Jesus at the feast of Passover, 14 Nisan, which corresponded with 25 March in the West and 6 April in the East. This date was thought in some Jewish traditions to be the date upon which the world was created, the patriarchs were born and the Exodus took place, and when the Day of the Lord would come at the close of history. As is widely known, the western Church now observes the December date for Christmas, while in the East the festival is celebrated in January. Its twelve-day duration may simply be the result of the notional time gap between these two dates.

It is becoming increasingly impossible to convince people that Christmas does not begin until 25 December and does not end until the festival of the Epiphany. Frequently it is only the lectionary that can emphasize the commemoration of the Christmas story, by means of its use of scripture during this period. However, the modern celebration of Christmas should not create the false impression that this festival ranks historically alongside the great festivals of Easter and Pentecost. That is not to say that its popularization is in any sense unfortunate. Indeed, the human desire to celebrate with a party captures the essence of Christ's down-to-earth nature and enlivens the dead time of the year with 'tidings of comfort and joy'. Appropriately then, it has been described as a stroke of sheer genius thus to have Christmas celebrated at the same time as 'pagan' mid-winter festivities.

The Christmas themes of incarnation and revelation do not stop on 6 January, however, but continue through the following season of **Epiphany**. The word means the 'showing forth' or 'manifestation' of

God to the world of mortals through the person of Jesus Christ who was divine and mortal. It is thus still celebrating the birth of Christ although its other important commemoration is the baptism of Christ: the first public identification of Jesus with the Father. This latter commemoration was lost in the western Church until more recently. The *Revised Common Lectionary* encourages us to keep the First Sunday of Epiphany as the Baptism of Christ and thus emphasizes an original aspect of the wider celebration. The season of Epiphany extends to the fortieth day after Christmas, which is the festival of the Presentation of Christ in the Temple on 2 February when Simeon described the Christ child as 'a light to lighten the Gentiles and to be the glory of thy people Israel'. These are fitting words with which to draw Epiphany to a close and begin the long walk to the Cross.

Just as Advent is extended backwards with a preparatory period of reflection on the theme of incarnation and judgement, so Lent is preceded with a similar period of time during which loose ends are tied up. Described as **Ordinary Time**, the day following the Presentation until Ash Wednesday has no particular themes or emphases. The Church of England, in adopting the *Revised Common Lectionary*, has noted the absence of good creation material in it and has rescued Creation Sunday (lost from the Ninth Sunday before Christmas in the *Alternative Service Book* of 1980) and placed it on the Second Sunday before Lent.

Lent was traditionally the period of time during which those adults awaiting baptism were required to undergo a period of preparation, penitence and fasting. This process of self-examination and self-denial led to reception into full membership of the Church at baptism on Easter Day. A possible desire to imitate the forty days which Christ spent in the wilderness tempted by the Devil – but without including Sundays which were never fast days – resulted in Lent beginning on a Wednesday. This became Ash Wednesday when the practice grew of imposing ashes on the foreheads of worshippers as a sign of mortality and thus of the need for penitence.

Holy Week is the culmination of this period of penitence but is itself part of a two-week period called **Passiontide**. This provides preparation for Palm Sunday – the first day of Holy Week – and avoids the concentration of the highly emotive themes of the Passion all into one week. However, as Palm Sunday is the day of the traditional reading of the Passion narrative, often in semi-dramatic form, Passion Sunday as the name of the Fifth Sunday of Lent is not appropriate. Holy Week proceeds in a form which serves as an important teaching device with the commemoration of Christ's entry into Jerusalem on Palm Sunday; the Last Supper and institution of Holy Communion on Maundy Thursday followed by the betrayal and arrest; the crucifixion and death of Christ on Good Friday; and the repose of the body of Christ in the tomb on Easter Eve.

Easter is the birthday of the Christian faith. St Paul reminds us that, without resurrection, our faith is nothing. Although the resurrection is celebrated Sunday by Sunday, or indeed whenever bread and wine are shared in the Eucharist, the festival of Easter is the big feast; it is the Christian Passover – indicated in the adjectival use of the word 'paschal'. As Lent was traditionally the period of preparation for adult baptism, so Easter was the principal occasion during the year when baptism was administered. The symbolism of entering Christ's death and resurrection through the waters of baptism enhances the celebration of Easter. Recent paschal liturgies have been designed to accommodate the renewal of baptismal vows, particularly where no actual baptisms are to take place. Vigils and services of light on Holy Saturday or Easter Eve are perfect settings for the admission of new Christians into the community of faith.

The period of Easter lasts for fifty days – a mark of Lukan influence upon the liturgical year. This time span is emphasized by the *Revised Common Lectionary*'s reference to Sundays *of* Easter rather than *after* Easter. Its lectionary material expounds the essential mystery of the redeeming work of Christ in his death and resurrection, and emphasizes the divine plan of the returning of the Son to the Father and the sending of the Holy Spirit at Pentecost – fifty days after Easter begins. As a result, Ascension Day is an integral part of Easter and not a festival which somehow marks the end of the Eastertide season. (The paschal candle should remain lit until Pentecost!) Nevertheless, lectionary material which follows Ascension Day begins to look towards the Holy Spirit theme of Pentecost.

If Advent is the birthday of the Christian year and Easter the birthday of the Christian faith, then **Pentecost** is the birthday of the Christian Church. The disciples are commissioned by the sending of the Holy Spirit to become apostles with power to continue Christ's work on earth through his Church. The word from the Greek indicates the 'fifty days' which elapsed between the Jewish Passover and the Pentecost festival of the wheat harvest. As Easter became the

Christian equivalent of Passover's celebration of redemption and salvation, so Pentecost was the appropriate name to adopt for the celebration of the sending of the Holy Spirit fifty days on from Easter Day. It was surely no coincidence that vast crowds were present in Jerusalem at the same time for the Jewish festival of Pentecost thus ensuring a large constituency for Peter's evangelism 'making disciples of all nations'. The Christian festival of Pentecost is also known as Whit Sunday – a name rapidly becoming disregarded as both missing the point and too quaintly Anglican.

The First Sunday after Pentecost is called Trinity Sunday and celebrates God as three persons in one: Father, Son and Holy Spirit. It has been described as a summary of all that has been commemorated in the Easter to Pentecost season. The long period of ordinary time which follows – up to the **Kingdom** season before Advent – is designated the **Sundays after Trinity**. This designation has a chequered history: the Sarum rite used such a description of these Sundays as does still the Book of Common Prayer. The *Alternative Service Book* of 1980 switched to the (until then) more common 'Sundays after Pentecost'. The *Revised Common Lectionary* has reverted to 'Sundays after Trinity' in keeping with increasing such usage in other parts of the Church. Thus the essential doctrine of the Christian faith is emphasized and given greater breadth of expression.

The shape of the Christian year is the bench-mark which shapes liturgy and lectionary. It celebrates, commemorates and teaches, while giving full expression to the worship of God which we offer to the Father in the Spirit through his Son Jesus Christ.

Michael Hampel

List of Abbreviations of Bible Translations Cited

JB   Jerusalem Bible
NEB   New English Bible
NIV   New International Version
NRSV   New Revised Standard Version
REB   Revised English Bible

Word Among Us

The First Sunday of Advent

Isaiah 2:1–5; Psalm 122; Romans 13:11–14; Matthew 24:36–44

The belief that the New Testament writers held, that God was king, or that his kingdom would one day be established, was neither new nor particularly startling. What they were excited about was the conviction that this kingdom had already begun to dawn, and that God was entering just now into human history. Not surprisingly, they believed that this would make a radical difference to the way things were. The whole point, however, was not the *reality* of God's kingly rule, but the *immediacy* of it.

The Hebrew prophets prepared the ground for such convictions. This passage from Isaiah was probably written at around the same time as chapters 40–55; later, that is, than most of the earlier chapters of the book. It is placed here to assert faith in what God will do 'in days to come', after the nation of Israel has been vindicated for all she has suffered and is restored again to her own land after exile in Babylon. Israel would then play her part in the councils of all the nations. The role of prophecy is complex. We may think that it is always concerned to predict the future. However, what it more important is that the prophet speaks God's words; someone once said that it is not so much *fore*-telling as *forth*-telling. What is more important still is that prophecies are recorded in texts, so that they have an effect upon the life and faith of contemporary readers, and do not simply recall what took place in the past.

The theme of Psalm 122 is linked to the same idea. This is a Psalm which was sung by pilgrims as they approached Jerusalem. Anyone who has stood overlooking that city reciting this Psalm cannot help but feel moved at the beauty and the theological resonance of the place, which can still seem to be the centre of the world. We who think such thoughts today are at the end of a long line of predecessors who 'pray for the peace of Jerusalem'.

From belief in the coming of God and from wonder at the sight of the holy city we move in Romans 13 to Paul's anticipation of the appearing of Jesus. This is the famous passage which brought about the conversion of St Augustine of Hippo, 'not in revelling and drunkenness, not in debauchery and licentiousness, not in quarrelling and jealousy. Instead, put on the Lord Jesus Christ.' This is the summons

1

to a life lived in the context of the eternal future offered to all people and known now by those who respond in faith to Jesus Christ.

Matthew 24 provides one of the basic texts for this complex of beliefs. Here is Jesus, towards the end of his life, warning his disciples that the end is to come imminently, and that the events which accompany its coming will be spectacular. The imagery is stark, deriving as it does from the apocalyptic tradition which provided the context for the preaching of Jesus. In a day when the actual beginning and end of history are matters of scientific exploration rather than theological dogma, we need to read through the words of Jesus to penetrate their essentials. Stripped down to these, the message is that any moment might reveal the glorious presence of the God who is Father of Jesus Christ.

What hope is there for the world? Can we look forward to anything, or are we condemned either to seeing things getting steadily worse or to an endless circularity of improvement and decline? The answer from Christian tradition has always been that hope can only truly be fixed in God. The proper response to him is one of goodness, kindness and compassion to our neighbour, such as God shows to us. These qualities can reveal the Christ who is gloriously present in our neighbour.

Application

Someone has said that to speak now of the return of the Lord Jesus is, for the present generation, to speak of our death.
* How do we work out appropriate ways of re-interpreting those elements of the New Testament message which are couched in terms unintelligible to our culture?
* And what attention do we give to the way we are to die?

The Second Sunday of Advent

Isaiah 11:1–10; Psalm 72:1–7, 18–19; Romans 15:4–13;
Matthew 3:1–12

Advent points us relentlessly towards the future. Yet we do well to remember that the past is important for Christian people. However, it is a past of engagement with its own past, so that we may find bearings for perceiving and meeting God who comes to us, as it were, out of the future.

This was the conviction of the prophet Isaiah. The picture he paints is no cosy romance for 'insiders'; it is a vision for all the nations of the world, who are called to live alongside one another in peace, justice and mutual celebration. Psalm 72 speaks of Israel's king and the people's hopes for him at the centre of God's plans for the whole world. The starting point may well be the nation of Israel, but Israel's hope extends to the whole world.

In Romans Paul states that the Hebrew scriptures were written for the instruction of Christian people, so that we may take our bearings from the way in which God had led his chosen people, the Jews, in ages past. These scriptures, says Paul, are to be read in the light of Christ, for he sums up the whole of Israel's history and hopes.

Christians today must be careful not to take this to mean that we can ride roughshod over Jewish hopes and religious aspirations. St Paul's views on biblical interpretation are not the last word! What it does mean, however, is that we have to understand Jesus in his context, as a first-century Jew, who cannot be understood apart from the religious history of his own people.

It is in the light of this that we have to read John the Baptist. The notion of 'preparing the way' comes from Isaiah 40, when the prophet sings of the way in which 'the way of the Lord' is to be prepared across the deserts which extend from Babylon to the land of Israel. The image is that of return from exile, and a road has to be built for the exiles who are returning. This means the levelling of mountains and the raising up of valleys to make a straight and even path. The prophet's concern, however, was not only that Israel should return from exile, but that God should return as well, so that the people's restored life in the land would from the very beginning be one centred in God.

3

Such is the background to John's status in Christian tradition as the one who 'prepares the way'. It is God who is to come – and Christian people see the coming of God in the coming of Jesus. This is the great restoration; but it is more than a restoration, for it is a beginning. What God is about to do is something new, for the end of all things will be the renewal of all things.

Everybody must prepare for this; hence the judgement on those who obstruct the ways of God and prevent the people's response; hence, too, the call to be ready to meet the one who is to come. The 'crisis' which is to come (that is the Greek word for 'judgement') will be a time for decision; are those who are to be confronted by Jesus going to accept or reject him and his message?

Application

In what ways does it make sense to speak of God's judgement today?

The Third Sunday of Advent

Isaiah 35:1–10; Psalm 146:4–9 *or* Luke 1:46b–55; James 5:7–10;
Matthew 11:2–11

The passage from Isaiah is to be dated from the time of the Exile, and what the prophet is promising is vindication with a difference. The people have suffered much, and God promises to make their future glorious. In a sense, this is recompense for all that they have had to endure; but it goes beyond that. The image set before the people is one of the absence of fear, of sight for the blind, of hearing for the deaf and of agility for the disabled. The prophet goes on to speak of a way back from Babylon through the desert, and then of peace, security and unity with all the created order when God returns with his people to the land he originally promised them.

Psalm 146 celebrates God, who is both Creator and Saviour of all. There is no distinction in the work of God; he both brings into being and puts things right. A similar theme is present in the Magnificat, though the thought there is developed even further. This hymn has much in common with the song of Hannah, the mother of Samuel, in 1 Samuel 2. But Mary takes Hannah's sentiments further. Hannah is content simply to note that God makes some poor and some rich, but Mary begins to set the work of human redemption within the context

Application

Passages such as these make us aware of the political implications of faith. From the days of John the Baptist through to the insights of 'Liberation Theology', there have been those who have noted that to believe in the God who is Father of Jesus Christ is to develop a vision for a new human society. The gospel is primarily political; individual, personal salvation is a feature of new social landscape. What attention do we give to social and political priorities in our preaching of the gospel?

of connections and mutuality; the poor are raised in dignity as the greatness of the rich is put into perspective. So the Epistle of James urges patience for those who are poor, for the coming of the Lord will put to right all the grievances and injustices of life.

It is not surprising that John the Baptist should doubt whether Jesus was 'the one who was to come'. According to the Gospel accounts he had announced that Jesus was the one whom his disciples should follow, but the kingdom of God had not yet dawned. John was in prison for offending an unjust king, and his cause was to end in his death. So he wondered whether he had got it right. 'Are you the one, or should we look for someone else?'

Jesus, ever the master teacher and never the dogmatist, does not answer the question directly but invites the messengers to look at what is going on. What they should be able to see is precisely what prophets foretold and Psalmists sang about: 'the blind receive their sight, the lame walk, the lepers are cleansed, the deaf hear, the dead are raised, and the poor have good news brought to them.' (All these things have taken place in the preceding chapters in Matthew's Gospel.) So Jesus challenges John's messengers (and thereby John himself) to consider the place of Jesus himself in the scheme of things: '. . . blessed is anyone who takes no offence at me.'

We do not know what John made of all this, but his place in the divine scheme of things was already assured. Because he fulfilled his calling to be the messenger who 'prepared the way' for God's coming, he is nothing less than the greatest among those born of women. But there is a further surprise, for even 'the least in the kingdom of heaven is greater than he'. What on earth can Jesus mean? We cannot be certain, but it seems that what is in store for those who respond to God's invitation to receive the promises of the kingdom of God will outdo, outstrip and outshine anything and everybody which went before. Our riches are great indeed!

The Fourth Sunday of Advent

Isaiah 7:10–16; Psalm 80:1–7, 17–19; Romans 1:1–7;
Matthew 1:18–25

It is unlikely that the prophet Isaiah consciously foretold the birth of Jesus. He was active in Jerusalem in the eighth century BC and spoke of what was significant to the rulers and people of that city. By referring to a 'young woman' who was pregnant, he was drawing the king's attention to the speed with which the purposes of God would be fulfilled. The name given to the child to be born to her was a sign that the child himself was to be a reminder of the presence of God. In particular, God was about to act speedily, and the measure of the child's growth was to be the measure of the time of God's activity among the people.

The Psalm captures one of the nuances of Israel's longing for vindication. The people are plunged into despair and long to know God's salvation. The particular prayer here is that God will be gracious to Israel's king and give him courage and victory. Such passages as these were taken up by the early Church and referred to Jesus.

It is possible that St Paul, at the beginning of his letter to the Romans, is quoting from an early Christian hymn or confession of faith, when he says of Jesus, 'who was descended from David according to the flesh and was declared to be Son of God with power according to the spirit of holiness by resurrection from the dead'. If that is so, then here is a very early assertion of the status of Jesus and his relationship with God the Father. Even if this is not the case, what is remarkable about it is the profundity of the simple opening of a letter in which Paul addresses his concerns to the Church at Rome.

A number of these themes come together in the simple story of the nativity of Jesus, as Matthew tells it. Mary was found to be pregnant before she had had any sexual relations with Joseph. He was not the kind of man to make a fuss, so he simply decided to break off the engagement. Divine intervention prevented him from doing so, and he married her and brought up Jesus as his own son. The angel's message includes the revelation that this child is a son of David, like his earthly father; he is also son of God, the fruit of the Holy Spirit.

His name is to be Jesus (meaning 'God is salvation'), and he is also to be known by the same name as the baby in the story about Isaiah, Emanuel, 'With-us-is-God'. Such a title foreshadows the immediacy and the imminence of God which is to feature later in the teaching of Jesus about God's kingdom.

With all these resonances of story and memories of a nation, with all this theological tradition, with all this expectancy, the story of the birth of Jesus is told. As we hear the story again over the next few days, we might consider the matter-of-fact way in which it is told, which seems to highlight its wonder; and the wonderful graciousness of God, who is known to us in the matter-of-fact things of earth, like birth, and love, and worry and kindness. All these virtues are the stuff of God's presence among us.

Interpretation

Matthew's constant concern is to show how the whole life of Jesus is a fulfilment of the promises made to Israel in the Hebrew scriptures – our 'Old Testament'. If we were to take our histories and the narratives of our past with equal seriousness, what are the occasions which we might identify as 'promises' made to us which were fulfilled later in our lives, as we grew older?

Christmas Eve

2 Samuel 7:1–5, 8–11, 16; Psalm 89:2, 21–27; Acts 13:16–26;
Luke 1:67–79

At first sight this is a curious set of readings for a celebration of
the Eucharist during the morning of Christmas Eve. Today of all
days, why set the story of David's desire to build a temple alongside a
missionary sermon of St Paul's in the Acts of the Apostles, with a
Psalm which celebrates the kingship of David?

On closer inspection, however, the readings may be seen to have a
subtlety which is quite appropriate at the threshold of this festival of
God's incarnation among us. The passage from 2 Samuel speaks of
David's desire to build a house, or temple, for God. He is initially
encouraged in this plan by the prophet Nathan. Subsequently, however, God reveals to Nathan that David is not to be the one who will
build a house for God, but God will build a house for him; in other
words, he will establish the Davidic dynasty among his people. 'Your
throne shall be established for ever,' he is told.

Psalm 89 echoes these words with the Psalmist's own exclamation,
'Your steadfast love is established for ever.' Nowhere was this more
eloquently seen than in God's faithfulness towards David. The Psalm

Application

For most of us Christmas comes with such a rush that
we hardly find the time to consider in peace and quiet
how it might affect the way in which we live our lives
during the remainder of the year. Given the degree to
which the Christmas story sums up much of Israel's hope
and expectation, what are there in our own lives of
details which might seem unconnected at first glance, but
which might be given more meaning in the light of
the presence of God with us in the person of this little
baby?

may have links with traditions related to Nathan's prophecy in 2 Samuel; it certainly celebrates God's faithfulness in his covenant relationship with David.

The preaching of Paul at Antioch in Pisidia in Acts 13 makes reference to a number of Old Testament characters, including David, whom God called 'a man after my own heart, who will carry out all my wishes'. It is from this religious heritage that Jesus was born.

The Gospel passage from Luke is the song which Zechariah sang at the circumcision of John the Baptist, who was to be the forerunner of Christ. Its central theme, again, is the faithfulness of God to what he has promised his people. The whole of their history is one of promised salvation; according to Zechariah, the time has come for all these promises to be fulfilled in the future which his son will herald and which the Son of God will perform.

Such is the sense of expectation, hope and joy on the morning of Christmas Eve.

Christmas Day

Isaiah 9:2–7; Psalm 96; Titus 2:11–14; Luke 2:1–14 *or* 1–20

The prophet Isaiah expresses the people's joy as their king gains victories for them against their enemies. Indeed, the victories are of such a kind that the people will always recall the story of Gideon routing the Midianites with a small number of warriors but with the supernatural help of God. The jubilant cry, 'for unto us a child is born' probably derives from the enthronement ritual of the king, when he was regarded as having that day become as the offspring of God.

The Psalm is one of praise to God, again for his victory; except that here victory is seen primarily as God's work of creation: '. . . as for all the gods of the nations, they are but idols; but it is the Lord who made the heavens.' The whole creation is to give thanks when God comes to visit the earth, for he will come with justice. This is not to say that he is coming to pass judgement in the legal sense on those who have 'done wrong'. Rather, he will administer political justice on behalf of those who have suffered unjustly.

The chosen passage from the Letter to Titus features a clear section of teaching. The context is one which urges right behaviour; and the basis upon which this is done is the recollection of the gracious acts of God in his sending of Jesus Christ. Those who await the coming of God are to exercise self-control; they are to live just and godly

---

Application

If the shepherds represent the outsiders, what are the ways in which the people of God today might learn of the grace of God given to those whom society rejects? Who are the outsiders in our contemporary community, society and world?

lives. These ethical themes are typical of the Pastoral Epistles, written by a disciple of Paul. They represent a time of 'settling down' to ordered existence in the world. It is as well to remember that the coming of Jesus may well present some disorder for our priorities.

So we come to the story of the nativity itself – with all the ingredients of the foregoing readings. Here is God as king, victorious on behalf of his people (glossed by Christians, in the light of the gospel, as the whole human race); here is the creator coming to save and vindicate his beloved creation; here is the source and motivation of all love come to urge, persuade and free us all to love both our neighbour and our God. And he comes to us as one of us, beyond us yet among us and within, to change our humdrum existence into the stuff on which angel songs are composed: peace in the highest, and glory upon earth.

Well may the shepherds wonder at what they see. They live almost as pariahs in their community, for the dirtiness of their work, and because of the risk of ritual taboo. Yet shepherds are one of the Bible's favourite metaphors for Godhead, kingship and the relationship which Jesus has with those who follow him. Humble though these men are, they are brought to see the greatest wonder of all: God's own son as a little baby. Their glory and praise is continued in the place and in the work to which they return.

Christmas Day

Second set of readings

Isaiah 62:6–12; Psalm 97; Titus 3:4–7; Luke 2:1–7 *or* 1–20

The passage from Isaiah is from the final and latest section of the book, after the Exiles have returned from Babylon. Here the promise is that they will receive the fruits of their labours and not have them taken from them, as is the case with slaves or exiles. Moreover, they will live at ease and at peace, knowing the goodness of God and experiencing his salvation. With their fortunes now reversed, they will truly be a 'City not forsaken'. This is the nature of the salvation promised to them.

The praises of God occupy the mind and thought of the Psalmist, for God is the creator of all things. For this reason creation itself praises God for his greatness; to his coming the earth responds in noisy adoration. The Psalmist is also conscious of the place of the people of God in God's purposes: by his choice of Israel God has made a people who can live before him and, by keeping the Law, which his grace has given to them, they are able to stand upright in his presence.

Titus refers to God's mercy being poured out in order to save us in Christ. For Christian people, it is the same grace that has brought Jesus Christ. Israel never was saved only because they did what God required; they were dependent upon his choice of them. In the same way Jesus was sent 'not because of any works of righteousness that we had done, but according to his mercy'.

What is also significant in the Epistle is the role it accords to the Holy Spirit, and we do well to consider this. It was God's Spirit who was active in creation, in prophecy, and in the conception of the son of God in the womb of Mary. It is not usual for the work of the Spirit to be accorded much prominence at Christmas time, but this theological imbalance could be to our loss.

St Luke's account of the nativity of the Lord is a story about outsiders being included in the purposes of God. The pregnant girl has not been abandoned by her fiancé, but accepted and loved; the couple have found shelter during the census, not in an inn, which was too full to accommodate them, but in a stable, where the manger forms the cradle of the son of God. Shepherds, regarded as outcasts and unclean by polite and pious society, are those to whom the story first comes. Already, therefore, we are coming across themes precious to St Luke's telling of the story of Jesus.

We do well to recall that these shepherds were ordinary people at work. The daily round is the place where we also shall discover that God is at work.

Application

The God and Father of Jesus Christ is to be discovered in the daily round of work, leisure and family life.
* How do we set about making ready for that discovery?
* What might we do to celebrate that presence in the context of our everyday work?

Christmas Day

Third set of readings

Isaiah 52:7–10; Psalm 98; Hebrews 1:1–4 *or* 1–12; John 1:1–14

The prophet takes an aesthetic delight in the image of the runner crossing all kinds of terrain in order to bring news of political or military nature: 'How beautiful upon the mountains are the feet of the messenger . . .' As each foot falls on the ground, so the news approaches, gradually coming nearer to those who need to hear it. The messenger is swift-footed, and the citizens of Jerusalem will sing out for joy when they hear what he has to say. Similarly the Psalmist calls for songs of joy at the wonderful deeds of God.

The writer to the Hebrews uses a different rhetorical device: not the vivid image but the persuasive character of contrast. He speaks of the high place of angels in Jewish history and worship, but says that Jesus is higher and better than they. In former times God spoke through the prophets, but now he has uttered a Son.

The theme is similar in the opening verses of St John's Gospel. But here it is elaborated still further, for the reference in these verses is not simply to the Hebrew scriptures, but to the whole tradition of thought which is current in the Hellenistic world at the time of this Gospel's writing. The Greek word which we translate 'Word' is *Logos*, and there is no one English word adequate for it, since it

Background

The word Logos is an elusive term, and we must beware of over-simplifying it. Not only are there echoes of the Wisdom literature in the Old Testament, but the expression also carries much of the meaning to be found in the work of Philo of Alexandria. For further reading, see Elizabeth Harris, 'Prologue and Gospel', *Journal for the Study of the New Testament* Supplement Series 107, Sheffield, 1994.

means the principle of creativity, the rationality of things, the dynamic of meaning, the force of life, and a whole lot more besides. These verses are the prologue to a great religious drama, in which all the characters and themes are assembled which will be explored throughout the rest of the book. What is important for today is that 'the Logos became flesh'.

The Logos was at work in the creation; he had his being alongside God and in God, and indeed was God. According to John, the Logos of God has assumed human flesh and come to live among his people. The drama will go on to indicate the conflict this creates, for there is a human tendency to prefer darkness to light, even though the light of life and truth is offered to us in this man.

Jesus, the Logos of God, presents himself to us and invites us to receive him. To those who do receive him he gives power and authority to become children of God, just as he is himself.

So St John says that Jesus sums up, not just Jewish hopes, but also all the Greek speculative thought of his day. This courageous re-casting of the context prompts us to ask how we are to express the pre-eminence of Jesus in terms contemporary with us.

The First Sunday of Christmas

Isaiah 63:7–9; Psalm 148; Hebrews 2:10–18; Matthew 2:13–23

The third and final section of the book of Isaiah, although it takes its name from the eighth-century Isaiah of Jerusalem, centres on the themes of 'afterwards'. The Exile which was prophesied by Isaiah himself has taken place; now the people have also experienced the return spoken of by Second Isaiah. The third section of the book of Isaiah speaks of the wonder of deliverance. This unknown prophet, conscious of writing in the tradition of the earlier Isaiah, is able to 'recount the gracious deeds of the Lord', because he and his contemporaries have known them for themselves. This message is desperately required by the inhabitants of Jerusalem, for they have discovered that their return to their homeland was not without its problems, and they are beginning to feel disheartened.

The language of 'recounting the gracious deeds' is developed in Psalm 148. God is the only God, the one creator of all things. He 'raised up strength for his people'; he has a particular regard for the children of Israel, and they know his special care. This care is extended to all people in Jesus Christ, and the Epistle to the Hebrews explores the truth that perfection comes through the experience of suffering. The incarnation looks forward to the cross, and it is by his sacrificial offering of himself as a grown man that this child will effect the salvation of all people. What is more, because he has

Application

It is not always easy to reflect on pain when all the world seems to be rejoicing – any more than it is easy to rejoice when we are aware that others are in pain. As we continue with our Christmas celebrations, why not set aside some time to think about and pray for those who are very ill, or who have suffered bereavement at this time of celebration?

suffered, even to the point of death, he is able to provide comfort, support and help to all who suffer.

The Gospel reading reminds us that there might be elements of human suffering that remain impervious to redemption. No number of repetitions of the claim could ever persuade the mothers of the murdered Holy Innocents that their cruel death was in any way 'good'. This story is a reminder against glibness in the face of appalling tragedy and evil. 'Unto us a son is given . . .', but from them were many daughters and sons taken away.

The story enables Matthew to apply a text about Israel's slavery in Egypt as a prophecy that Jesus, too, must have gone there and returned; and we are told in Exodus both of Pharaoh's plan to kill the Israelite children, and of the killing of the first-born of the Egyptians.

A further text is taken to be fulfilled in Joseph's taking his wife and son to Nazareth, so that the child 'may be called a Nazarene'. Where this text comes from is not altogether clear. Maybe it is an allusion to Isaiah 11, where the word for 'branch' is *neitzer*; or, since Nazarenes were despised, as St Jerome suggested, there may be a reference here to the fact that Jesus will be despised and rejected by his people.

Such use of texts may appear to be merely playing and a superficial avoidance of the real issues that underlie these passages, such as the anguish of the parents of the murdered children, and the comparable suffering today on the part of millions who see their children killed by violence, famine or disease. That danger always exists. However, first, the placing of human pain in the broader context of a religious tradition has always been the one way of integrating it into life; and second, the gospel is not and never has been about the avoidance of pain, even of the most excruciating kind. What it provides is a way of offering it and understanding it as part of the great mystery of the ways of God with humankind. We are invited to look forward to a redemption yet to come. That redemption may not yet be visible, but what may be visible to the eye of our spirits is the son of Mary, the Son of God, who is with us in all pain and intends to remain with us until we all come to glory. The incarnation cannot avoid the cross.

The Second Sunday of Christmas

Jeremiah 31:7–14 *with* Psalm 147:12–20; *or* Ecclesiasticus 24:1–12 *with* Wisdom of Solomon 10:15–21; Ephesians 1:3–14; John 1:1–9 *or* 1–18

Jeremiah was the prophet of doom; we still speak (well, some do!) of a 'jeremiad'. Yet here the prophet is promising return. God's prophecies always come with God's promises, in order to function as warnings of the inevitable, rather than as threats from a capricious God. After judgement and exile God will bring the people back. They will come from all the parts of the earth to which they have been scattered, and they will know that God's goodness to them is ever new. Once returned, they will live prosperously in their own land once more.

Alongside the prophecy, in Psalm 147, comes a further celebration of God's gracious activity, first in the wide and general sweep of creation, then in the detail of salvation for his people.

The 'Wisdom' options lead our thoughts in a different direction.

Application

In the light of these passages we are invited to engage, first, our hearts, as we worship this holy Jesus. The study of the scriptures moves us to a deeper love for God who has so wonderfully revealed his love to us. Second, as we think, with the aid of all our critical faculties, of what his coming means, we are reminded that our minds are also the creation of God. We do him no service if we refuse to use them to explore these central tenets of our humanity. Third, we need to remember that love and thought are nothing if they do not issue in a lifestyle which has holiness as its aim. Those who consider themselves disciples of Jesus will allow the gospel to address our will and our lifestyle.

This is perhaps the closest that the Jewish tradition comes to speculating in the abstract about the nature of reality. 'Wisdom' literature probably arose in the court of Solomon as those with the leisure and ability to write reflected upon the nature of life. This reflection was later brought more into line with the mainstream of Jewish faith, and 'Wisdom' was regarded as an agent of God, who took her place alongside God in the work of creation. Here in Ecclesiasticus she is seen as taking up residence, specifically, among the people of Israel.

Thus the Wisdom of Solomon can sing of Wisdom's role as God's agent in leading Israel out of slavery in Egypt, taking them through the Red Sea and giving them the gift of song.

The theme of God's activity before the world's creation is taken up again in Ephesians 1. Here we read of God's eternal purposes, which are focused in Christ. God blessed the whole human race in Christ, by choosing not just Israel, but also Gentiles, to be his own people; by redeeming them by the blood of Christ in forgiving their sin; and by giving his Holy Spirit to them as a promise of what was yet to come when the 'summing up' of all things is complete.

St John develops all these themes further as he teaches that the eternal Logos, who is the Word, the Wisdom, and the creative and rational principle of God, became flesh in the person of Jesus. So this time between Christmas and Epiphany provides us with ample material for reflection upon the ways of God with humanity.

The Epiphany

Isaiah 60:1–6; Psalm 72:1–7, 10–15 *or* 1–15; Ephesians 3:1–12; Matthew 2:1–12

'Life must go on.' And, after the celebration of Christmas, faith must go on. It must go on to behaviour, and it must go on to reflection.

The third section of the book of Isaiah, chapters 56–66, comprises prophecies to the city of Jerusalem which apply after the nation's return from exile in Babylon. 'Nations shall come to your light and kings to the brightness of your dawn,' it says; because of God's goodness to Israel in returning the people from exile to the holy city, Jerusalem is seen as the centre of the earth, the focus of God's attentions in the world. This theme is developed in Psalm 72; kings are not only the rulers of their people; they also represent them. So if kings come to visit and pay honour to the city, then the whole nation acknowledges its worth and beauty.

The wise men who came to visit the infant Jesus came in response to something which was disclosed to them; it is a common feature of religious understanding that it is God himself who reveals himself to the group or the individual, for the unaided individual or community needs to have its darkened understanding enlightened. The writer to the Ephesians, probably a disciple of Paul rather than the apostle himself, understands Paul's presentation of the gospel to the Gentiles in this way. Paul is shown here as the great emissary, or apostle, entrusted with the message of Christ; the Spirit of God is the agent and director of Paul's mission.

The coming to Jerusalem of the wise men from the east is one of the major and most marvellous stories in Christian tradition. In Christian art the wise men are variously seen to be scholars, astrologers, magicians and kings. Christian tradition sees them develop to the point at which they come to represent all nations, all ethnic groups and all parts of the earth. Their gifts are the gifts of wealthy nations. Only later did those gifts come to be associated with wealth, divinity and embalming; originally they symbolized the high value of the gifts which it is appropriate to offer to God.

The disappearance of the wise men from the narrative is much swifter than their arrival; as far as the narrative is concerned, they have played their part in the story simply by responding to the star, by coming and by worshipping. T. S. Eliot's poem *The Coming of the Magi* has them 'no longer at ease in the old dispensation'; they go back changed. The dream warning them not to return to Herod raises in the reader's mind, in the light of Herod's intentions, the question as to whether they have come for a birth or a death. This birth will issue in a death, but that death will lead to eternal life – for them, wherever they returned; for us, wherever our turning points; and for all.

Application

What does it mean for us to 'offer gifts' to God? How might we ensure that the offering we make of our lives is not simply an excuse for a refusal to allow our faith to affect our lifestyle and the economic and financial choices we make. To offer gifts to God is to give, in material terms, our money and our time to the service of God and our neighbour. The wise men's journey 'from the east' would have been costly!

The Baptism of Christ

The First Sunday of Epiphany

Isaiah 42:1–9; Psalm 29; Acts 10:34–43; Matthew 3:13–17

The distinctive feature of the Christian understanding of God is that what is divine comes to full expression in a human being. The belief that Jesus is the eternal Son of God, the second Person of the divine Trinity, involves the implication that whatever is human may be the bearer of the divine; so fully is Christ divine and so completely is he human that the whole of humanity is deified, just as the whole of God came to be a human person.

As a man of his time, responding to God, Jesus was baptized, 'in order to fulfil all righteousness'. That John should be baptized by him is more fitting, according to Matthew, from the viewpoint of abstract principle; but from the standpoint of one determined to do the will of God, it is Jesus who should submit to a ritual washing by John. We might paraphrase, 'in order to ensure that I do perfectly what is completely right.' The Spirit of God affirms this decision by expressing his approval and by adding the sprinkling of his own words of commendation. The king is adopted as a son at his crowning (Psalms 2, 110); the Son of God, who is also son of Mary (and, as is thought, of Joseph) is acclaimed by God as his own faithful and obedient heir.

We are invited to understand this baptized Christ as the anointed one of Israel, God's servant, who brings justice to the nations. The prophet glosses this as sight for the blind and release for prisoners. Jesus is the king, who embodies the nations and who will act in justice and usher in a new age of peace, when exile is a thing of the past, and when new things happen both in creation and in human dealings. The God who acts thus is worthy of the praise ascribed to him by the Psalmist. He speaks, and worlds obey him, for he is the power at work bringing them into being.

Peter's address in the house of Cornelius was given in response to God's giving the Spirit to Gentiles, in spite of Peter's initial doubts (Acts 9). The baptism of Jesus marked him out as God's chosen one, and he is now the object of the apostle's preaching, the one in whom all nations should trust and the one to whom all the prophecies point which are contained in the Hebrew scriptures. The exciting thing about this is that here is the God of Israel setting out to fulfil his own promise that all nations, all people, may be the inheritors of his promises to Israel. In other words, his chosen people is now to be regarded not just as the nation of Israel, but as the whole human race.

The infant Church found this a difficult lesson to learn, but learn it they did. We have the story of Cornelius as the great example of how the Church is called to leap across all boundaries that separate people from one another, so that all may find their unity as human beings in the body of Jesus, who is the son of the one God of all.

Background

The theme of kingship in the Hebrew scriptures makes for a fascinating study, for the idea that God is king over his people (cf. Psalms 93, 96, 97) mingles with the stories of the desire of the nation of Israel to have a king, and all the ambivalence about that (1 Samuel 8), with the clear teaching that David is chosen by God to be king (1 Samuel 16). This is the background to the theme of Jesus being the 'Son of God', and therefore king of Israel.

The Second Sunday of Epiphany

Isaiah 49:1–7; Psalm 40:1–11; 1 Corinthians 1:1–9; John 1:29–42

The Old Testament reading is one of the 'Servant Songs' in what is known as Deutero-Isaiah, the section of the Book of Isaiah which comprises chapters 40–55. The prophet speaks of this mysterious character – sometimes associated with the nation of Israel, sometimes very much an individual, maybe even the prophet himself; sometimes not so much the nation as one who acts on behalf of God towards the nation – who is God's 'servant'. This person will not only effect the restoration of Israel, now scattered among the nations of the earth; he will also cause all those nations to pay attention to Israel's God.

The Psalmist sings as one who also does God's will. He has known God's mercy ('He lifted me up out of the desolate pit, out of the mire and clay . . .') and is now concerned to do God's bidding. He has the insight to perceive that, far more important than all the ritual commandments – which God himself had given – are those commandments which have to do with speaking boldly of God's faithfulness and obeying God's command to live in faithful obedience to what God requires.

These Old Testament passages form the background to St Paul's opening words to the Church at Corinth. He gives thanks to God for his faithfulness, which extends to his ensuring that the Corinthians themselves remain faithful to their calling, to their faith and to their God.

Application

It is a remarkable feature of what little we know of John the Baptist that he was more than content for his followers to leave him and follow Jesus. Such selflessness may come as a challenge to our desire to hold on to our relationships for the sake of the self-esteem they provide for us.

St John records the baptism of Jesus obliquely, not in a narrative, but in John the Baptist's testimony. What is important is that the Spirit of God descended upon Jesus, for this is a sign that Jesus himself will baptize with the Holy Spirit. The story continues with the call of the first disciples. John the Baptist has already declared Jesus to be the 'Lamb of God, who takes away the sin of the world'; now he draws attention to him again, and this has the effect of making his own disciples switch their allegiance from John himself to Jesus. The significance of their visiting where he lives, or 'abides', may be to draw attention to the statement in the Gospel that he will 'abide' in his disciples (John 15). For John, discipleship comprises both being indwelt by and abiding in Jesus, in whom alone is the forgiveness of sins. These disciples will follow him and learn that his vocation is to do battle with the powers of darkness; they too will have to share in that.

The Third Sunday of Epiphany

Isaiah 9:1–4; Psalm 27:1, 4–9; 1 Corinthians 1:10–18;
Matthew 4:12–23

Isaiah 9 contrasts the experience of defeat with a coming time of victory and vindication. A similar theme is found in Psalm 27, in which the Psalmist is led to praise and thank God and to express his desire to remain in God's company at worship; only thus will he be sure of God's salvation. The prayer continues for an ever-growing sense of God's mercies and deliverance. Even though the Psalmist has known God's salvation, the danger of which he is afraid remains an ever-present threat, and he will need further deliverance in the future.

The reading begun last week is continued by 1 Corinthians, and here Paul begins to address the divisions of the Church in that city. The point is that, whereas the divided Christians insist on their allegiance to their party leader (as they understand Paul, Cephas and Apollos to be), Paul points out that these men are simply agents of Christ. The punctuation of the passage most sensibly should read as though Paul is countering their party slogans with the assertion, 'I am Christ's; is Christ divided?' Central to their unity is their baptism, and this baptism is into Christ. Among other implications, baptism implies the cross. What is important, as far as Paul is concerned, is

Application

Such is the nature of the baptism to which Christians are called; the unity of the Church, which Paul understands as rooted in baptism into the death of Jesus, is a unity of suffering offered to God for him to sanctify; perhaps this is why it is so often the persecuted churches which find a unity which goes deeper than mere agreement on formulae. How are we to keep a fervent faith alive for ourselves?

not who did the baptizing, but who did the saving; what matters is whether the baptized are conscious of Christ crucified at the centre of their faith.

Matthew 4 takes up the prophecy from Isaiah which we have just read; it sees the ministry of Jesus in Galilee as a fulfilment of that prophecy. Galilee is regarded as Gentile country, and the light the Gentiles see is the light of Jesus's preaching of the coming reign of God. It is in this context that Jesus calls his disciples. The promise is of light, but the present is darkness; the call is to sacrifice, not to honour; and the implications are nothing cosy, for they cost a livelihood.

The Fourth Sunday of Epiphany

1 Kings 17:8–16; Psalm 36:5–10; 1 Corinthians 1:18–31;
John 2:1–11

The touching story of the widow of Zarephath in 1 Kings 17 is among the most moving in the Old Testament. Elijah has just appeared before Ahab to tell him that, because of his idolatry, God is going to shut up the heavens and cause a drought. This presents a practical problem for the prophet, for even God's messengers need to eat and drink. The solution to the quandary is to be provided by a miracle that will continue until the rains return. However, it requires faith, not just on the part of Elijah, but also on the part of the widow who is to be his landlady. She has to use her last remaining flour to bake for him first; but she does it, and the promise of God's provision stands firm.

After an Old Testament reading about the withholding of rain there is something almost surreal in the choice of a Psalm which begins with the assertion that God's faithfulness 'reaches to the clouds'. Moreover, its message seems a little harsh for those who are beyond the confines of 'those who know you'. However, this is a celebration of those who are conscious of God's presence; they perceive and interpret their world in the light of this awareness of him. Therefore they cannot but offer him their praise.

Theology

Today we would probably not want to be as dismissive as Paul of those who ask us to demonstrate how our faith might stand up to the tests to which the Corinthians' faith is subject; it is, after all, only reasonable that enquirers should have their questions answered which demand evidence for belief and cogency in moral and religious argument. How well equipped are we to defend our faith in the face of the very real challenges it faces among the philosophies of our contemporary cultures?

St Paul's first letter to the Corinthians continues from last week the theme of the centrality of the cross in the life and lifestyle of believers. Against the demand from Jews for signs and proofs and from Greeks for wisdom and detachment, God in Christ offers passion – in two senses. In the literal sense, God in Christ undergoes, or suffers, what is done to him; in the metaphorical sense, we are confronted with God's passionate love, which leaps the barriers of unbelief and refusal to respond.

These themes are similar in John, though the language is different. The background to John's thought is the whole hellenistic world in which the gospel was first proclaimed; and at its centre is the glory of God active in the person of Jesus. All the Gospel's themes are set out in the Prologue. The story of Jesus and his disciples at the wedding in Cana is, according to the Evangelist, the first occasion on which he shows his glory – and the disciples believe in him right from the start. They will come to see, as will the reader of this remarkable text, that his glory is to be found chiefly in his crucifixion, and that what is true for him is true also for all who would follow him.

The Presentation of Christ in the Temple

Candlemas

Malachi 3:1–5; Psalm 24:1–6 *or* 1–10; Hebrews 2:14–18;
Luke 2:22–40

The Feast of the Presentation of Christ carries a number of themes. It marks the story of Mary and Joseph's going up to the Temple to fulfil the Law's requirements for the purification of a woman after childbirth, for the process made her ritually unclean. It also marks again an Epiphany theme, with Simeon both proclaiming the significance of Jesus for the Gentiles and prophesying the cross. For the Church, it marks the end of the period in the year, starting in Advent, in which we celebrate the incarnation of God in the person of Jesus.

The reading from Malachi, because it is quoted at the beginning of the first three Gospels with reference to John the Baptist, tends to make us want to refer the prophecy to him. In its origin it should be read without such conditioning; it speaks simply of God's coming to his Temple, after he has been absent during the nation's Exile, and that his return will be proceeded by a herald, or messenger. The theme of judgement is here, as are the themes of purification and offering. Judgement begins at the house of God, so that worship may be pure. That is why purification is necessary, not just after the ritual defilement of childbirth (and we must question today the pertinence of this and other Old Testament taboos), but for all people, whose motives may be mixed, whose lives are compromised and whose goals for holy living are frequently missed.

The Psalm takes up the theme of worship in a great song of entry into the Temple. The whole earth belongs to God, and it is to this God that the pilgrims advance in faith, adoration and expectation. But there are conditions to that approach, for only the pure may come to God. As God's people, we approach him now as the Temple which is the body of Christ. As he makes his entrance, so do we, for his life is lived in us, as is ours in him. The alternative Psalm, 84, sings of the beauty of the Temple, where God's goodness is known, and in which his people know his blessing.

The vivid imagery of Hebrews speaks of the high priesthood of Christ. He comes to the Temple to offer atonement for the sins of the

31

people; what he offers, however, is his own body, and that sacrifice aligns him with those on whose behalf he offers himself, for he has suffered whatever they suffer.

The story of Simeon and Anna is one of the most beautiful in scripture. These old people, one man, one woman, both devout, have much to teach about the virtue of looking forward to the new age of God's future. Simeon speaks of fulfilment, and Anna does the work of a preacher, pointing out the continuities between scripture and current events, and raising the hopes and wills of the hearers. Sight, light and insight are all here, and all for the Gentiles, all nations of the earth, so that they may see and respond to the good news of the presence of Jesus among humankind.

Background

There is much to be gained from a study of the relationship between Jesus and the Temple. Here he comes because he is brought by his parents, in obedience to the command in Leviticus 2:1–8. Later he will be found by his parents, while still a boy, listening to the elders in the Temple and asking them questions (Luke 2:46). One of his temptations was that he might throw himself down from its pinnacle (Luke 4:9). He spoke of a Pharisee and tax collector who went to the Temple to pray (Luke 18:10), and he demonstrated God's judgement against the Temple by overturning the tables of money-changers (Luke 19:45ff). His teaching in Jerusalem at the end of his life was frequently in the Temple, and its curtain between the Holy of Holies and the Holy Place was torn in two when he died (Luke 23:45). The Temple was so central to the life of Judaism that the earliest disciples came to understand Jesus as the embodiment of the Temple after it had been destroyed, and that the Christian community itself was its only rightful successor (cf. Ephesians 3:21–22).

Ordinary Time – Proper 1

Sunday between 3 and 9 February

Isaiah 58:1–9a *or* 1–12; Psalm 112:1–9 *or* 1–10;
1 Corinthians 2:1–12 *or* 1–16; Matthew 5:13–20

The prophet's concern is clear. Around him he sees spiritual life which is just a sham: much outward activity and show of devotion, such as fasting, and much apparent concern to know God and his ways, but it all turns out to be surface show, with no inner reality. What explodes this bubble of unreal spirituality is exploitation, quarrelling, and obvious lack of care for the poor and weak. Isaiah refuses to let us lock our relationship with God into a corner where we can enjoy him privately. True spiritual life is expressed first of all by defending the defenceless: fighting injustice, feeding the hungry, housing the homeless, clothing the naked. 'Then your light will break forth like the dawn', he says. 'Then you will call, and the Lord will answer!'

This is Jesus's concern also, in our Gospel reading. His disciples

Background

Salt that loses its taste? Strictly speaking, of course, salt cannot lose its taste. So Jesus's picture must draw on some way in which salt becomes so diluted that it is no longer any use except as a paving material (Matthew 5:13). Of the many explanations, the best pictures a pile of rock salt left beside a field. Every year, in very small quantities, this would be spread on the land to enhance fertility. But rain would gradually leech the salt out of the pile, until eventually it would lose its effectiveness. Then the gravelly material would be ideal to spread along the path beside the field.

Jesus's picture, therefore, is of his followers being spread out to influence the world around. Gathered into a heap by themselves, they are useless – like a lamp under a basket (5:15).

33

will shine as 'the light of the world' when people see their 'good deeds' and 'give glory to your Father in heaven'. They will be 'the salt of the earth' – a picture of preserving, protecting the world from corruption, and probably also of fertilizing, enabling the world to bring forth good fruit instead of bad. How does the Church today match up to this joint vision of Isaiah and of Jesus?

This will involve, says Jesus, a righteousness greater than that of the scribes and Pharisees. These were admired by everyone for their devotion, learning and strict obedience to all the requirements of the Law. Having to be more righteous than the Pharisees would have seemed impossible to all Jesus's hearers, including his disciples. In what way could their righteousness be surpassed? Jesus gives the answer when he calls his disciples 'salt of the earth' and 'light of the world'. The Pharisees restricted their sphere of 'righteousness' to the chosen people, Israel. They cared for the poor, certainly – but only the poor of their own people. Jesus expects more: an undiscriminating love which reaches out to all in need, regardless of race or religious qualification. This kind of love is what God's Law is all about, fulfilled now by Jesus.

And Paul shows us this love in practice. He tells the Corinthians how difficult it was for him to bring the good news of Christ to them.

Background

Paul's attitude towards persuasive words of wisdom (1 Corinthians 2:4) is remarkable, within the culture of the time. Rhetoric was a widely-taught and much-prized skill. People – especially those of high or rising social status – would pay to attend courses, in order to improve their chances of success in litigation (cf. 1 Corinthians 6:1–8) or in the city assembly. Paul refuses to associate himself with all of this, and deliberately preaches in a way which reveals his weakness. This technique, of course, matches the message, for he could hardly use rhetorical techniques associated with the powerful, and with power-play, in order to tell how God had chosen what is weak in the world to shame the strong (1 Corinthians 1:27).

He came 'in weakness and fear, and with much trembling'. But he felt driven by the Spirit to cross the racial barrier into the Corinthians' Greek culture, to reach out to them not just with social concern but with the message on which it rests, the secret 'wisdom of God' now revealed in Christ.

How can the Church of Jesus Christ have a true, deep spirituality which shines a bright beam of mercy into a dark world? The answer is a true, deep experience of the Spirit, such as Paul describes in our Epistle reading. A spirituality resting on such an experience will not be mere show, but a real sharing in the life of God himself, reaching out to the needs of the world.

Application

This prompts questions on styles of church life and methods of evangelism today. What kind of match is there between our buildings, our liturgies, our publications and our leadership structures, on the one hand, and the gospel of the boundary-crossing love of God in Christ for sinners, on the other? Is the message undermined by the medium?

Ordinary Time – Proper 2

Sunday between 10 and 16 February

Deuteronomy 30:15–20 *or* Ecclesiasticus 15:15–20; Psalm 119:1–8;
1 Corinthians 3:1–9; Matthew 5:21–37

In our Deuteronomy reading we meet Moses near the end of his life, making a final appeal to the Israelites. We might have thought that they would have little difficulty making the choice he puts before them. Who would choose death, rather than life? But we must not forget the awful attractiveness of idolatry. Instead of slow and

---

Theology

Jesus's teaching on divorce (Matthew 5:31–32; 19:3–9) needs careful thought. It must be set into its social and religious context in first-century Judaism. The giving of a certificate of divorce (5:31; 19:7) refers to a practice based on Deuteronomy 24:1–4: if a husband found something objectionable in his wife (Deuteronomy 24:1; NRSV), he could divorce her just by writing a certificate of dismissal and compelling her to leave his house. The Rabbis debated the meaning of the vague phrase 'something objectionable'. Some (the school of Shammai) defined it strictly as adultery or serious sexual sin, but others (the school of Hillel) gave it a much broader reference. The famous Rabbi Akiba even allowed 'something objectionable' to mean less pretty than another woman. It naturally suited men to allow themselves considerable freedom, and so it is not surprising that divorce was common in Jesus's day. Even his disciples were horrified by Jesus's much stricter teaching (Matthew 19:10). They felt that Jesus's apparent prohibition both of divorce and of remarriage effectively made marriage impossible!

Christian moral theology has generally maintained an absolutist view of marriage on the basis of Jesus's teaching:

---

difficult obedience, idolatry offers a quick fix. Worship me, says the god, and you'll find the quick route to sexual conquest, big harvests, victory over rivals and enemies, security and prosperity. But that way, Moses tells them, is the way of death.

Jesus too wants to protect his disciples from the way of death – from losing themselves in the fire of hell (vv. 22, 30), from ultimate judgement (v. 26). But now the way to life is not the Law of Moses, but Jesus's own teaching. In these so-called 'antitheses' Jesus opposes his words to the old teaching. The first is typical: 'you have heard that it was said to the people of old, "Do not murder" . . . but I say to you, Everyone who is angry with his brother is liable to God's judgement.'

Jesus makes anger as bad as murder, turns lust and remarriage

---

namely, that marriage is an indissoluble lifelong commitment, sealed by God, so that remarriage during the lifetime of a former partner is essentially adultery. The Eastern Orthodox tradition, however, does not take such a strict view, allowing divorce and remarriage up to three times.

In assessing the biblical roots of the issue, a vital question is to ask whether Jesus intended to annul the Mosaic permission of Deuteronomy 24. He certainly intended to limit its application, but his comment that it was given because 'you were so hard-hearted' (Matthew 19:8) suggests that he admitted its necessity – reluctantly. Hearts are still hard. And while Jesus elsewhere extends Old Testament law, this would be the only case in which, effectively, he would be saying that Moses was wrong – he should never have given you this law. In the face of what he sees as the flagrant abuse of the Mosaic permission – frequently leading to terrible suffering for women, forcing them into second marriages out of economic necessity – Jesus underlines God's original intention: a one-flesh union which cannot be torn apart without great damage to both parts. But the permission remains, hedged about with these warnings, to apply to those cases where hardness of heart wins the day. Interacting with Jesus's teaching, Paul confirms this view in 1 Corinthians 7:10–16.

after divorce into adultery, condemns all oath-taking as 'from the evil one' – and makes God's judgement hang upon people's response to this re-writing of the Law by him. Jesus steps into Moses's shoes and directs us to the way of life. Behaviour contrary to his teaching will lead to death, not life.

There is probably truth in the view that Moses would not have been too upset by this stiffening of his commandments, because Jesus is actually drawing out their inner intention and real meaning. At any rate, it is interesting that the things Jesus opposes are all at the heart of idolatry, both ancient and modern. Idolatry is to do with power – how to get rich, get health, get pleasure, get rid of your enemies. It thus sharpens rivalries, turns people into sex objects and makes them dispensable, and above all corrupts speech, making any lie worthwhile if it brings the desired success.

Jesus's way is so different. Instead of rivalry, reconciliation. Instead of lust and exploitation, love and faithfulness. Instead of pretentious word-waving, simple truthfulness. Reconciliation, he says, is the indispensable foundation of all true worship. If a relationship needs repairing, then give that an absolute priority: leave your gift before the altar, and sort it out.

They needed to do this in Corinth. There the church had fallen into factions, marked by 'jealousy and quarrelling'. They thought that they were standing up for spiritual principle, by supporting the teacher who had got it right: 'I follow Paul', 'I follow Apollos'. There may have been two other groups, following 'Christ' and 'Peter' (see 1 Corinthians 1:12) – or, after drawing attention to all this division, Paul may be insisting on the oneness of Christ. But the point remains that he sees disunity as an infection of worldliness, no better than the pagan Corinthians who promoted the worship of their 'favourite' god. Idolatry can attack us in the most subtle ways.

Ordinary Time – Proper 3

Sunday between 17 and 23 February

Leviticus 19:1–2, 9–18; Psalm 119:33–40;
1 Corinthians 3:10–11, 16–23; Matthew 5:38–48

The reading from Leviticus 19 has been chosen to go with our Gospel passage from Matthew 5. However, 'love your neighbour' in Leviticus 19:18 looks rather different from 'love your enemies' in Matthew. Is Jesus sharpening up the Law of Moses again, extending the definition of 'neighbour' to include the very last people we would put into that category? We remember how he answered the question 'Who is my neighbour?' by telling the parable of the Good Samaritan (Luke 10:29–37).

But actually the fundamental principles are the same in both passages. Leviticus 19 begins with 'Be holy, because I, the Lord your God, am holy.' Matthew 5 ends with 'Be perfect, therefore, as your heavenly Father is perfect.' And the repeated 'I am the Lord' in Leviticus reminds the Israelites why they must leave windfalls for the poor, not swear, not tease the defenceless, and not endanger others but love their neighbour as themselves: because this behaviour matches the character of their God. 'I am the Lord' is the completely sufficient argument: if they live this way, they will live in friendship with him. In just the same way, Jesus tells us that those who love their enemies will be 'sons and daughters of your father in heaven', for he pours his goodness indiscriminately on all, good and bad alike. They will bear the family likeness.

But what a difficult instruction is attached to this principle! 'Love your enemies and pray for those who persecute you' is challenging enough, but 'Do not resist an evil person . . . turn the other cheek' seems not only impossible but even unwise. What can Jesus mean? Three points help understanding here:

1. Love is truly the fundamental idea, and we must not tone down its implications. Inspired by the love of God for his enemies, we are to imitate him. In our New Testament reading Paul reminds us how this is possible: only through the indwelling Holy Spirit.

2. The five instructions introduced by 'Do not resist an evil person' are in descending order of seriousness – from the foul insult of a slap on the face, to someone who wants a loan. In between Jesus pictures two situations which his hearers must often have seen: a poor man losing his cloak in payment of a debt (although this was forbidden by the Law), and a Roman soldier forcing a civilian to carry his pack.

Text / Doctrine / Application

'Love your neighbour as yourself' Leviticus 19:18. Dr Gordon Wenham comments that love and neighbour are as wide-ranging in their scope and meaning in Hebrew as are the corresponding English terms, and thus that Jesus and Paul were not stretching the meaning of these verses in claiming that all our other duties towards our fellow men were summed up in this command. Wenham has Matthew 22:39–40 and Romans 13:9 in mind, but in fact this is one of the most-quoted verses: see also Matthew 19:19, Mark 12:33, Galatians 5:14, Ephesians 5:28 and James 2:8, as well as Matthew 5:43 in today's Gospel. Contemporary Jewish thinking tended to identify neighbour as fellow Jew: for instance, the members of the Qumran community were commanded to love all the sons of light (that is, members of the community), and hate all the sons of darkness (that is, all who oppose them, and all Gentiles). But Jesus radically extended neighbour to include not just Gentiles, but even enemies.

In reflecting on love . . . as yourself, it is surely right to note that there is a healthy self-love at the heart of Christian spirituality, even though in its essence Christian love is self-forgetful. This paradox arises because those who live with, or suppress, feelings of self-loathing or rejection will be hampered in their ability to love others freely. They will tend either to idealize others – turning them into the self they wish they were – or to see them as rivals for the status and admiration by which they try to compensate for their own feelings. Either way, true self-forgetful love is impossible, because our actions and styles of relating are motivated by our own inner needs. To learn to love ourselves as the objects of God's love – as enemies so prized by Christ that he was willing to die for us – is the essential starting-point for the expression of that same love towards others.

3. In each case Jesus gives instructions about his disciples' response. These instructions are not laws, but what the American scholar Robert Tannehill has called 'focal instances' – little snapshot examples of what love might call us to do. The challenge is this: in every situation of conflict, whether serious or trivial, how may I best love the person who insults me, exploits me, uses me? The answer cannot be prescribed in advance – but by his illustrations Jesus shows that such love needs to be creative, surprising, and self-sacrificial. The Roman soldier who press-gangs a passer-by into carrying his pack will be shocked to be met not by resentment but by genuine interest – questions about his family, sympathy about separation from home and the hardships of military life, warm conversation which extends until suddenly two miles have been covered, rather than one.

This love bears the hallmark of divine likeness. It may look dove-like and be mobbed by the hawks, but it will be owned by the God who loves the unlovely.

The Second Sunday before Lent

Genesis 1:1–2:3; Psalm 136 *or* Psalm 136:1–9, 23–26;
Romans 8:18–25; Matthew 6:25–34

The readings all cluster around the theme of Creation, taking their lead from today's beautiful Gospel. The creation story in Genesis 1 sets the scene by presenting two balancing truths which are then picked up in Matthew 6 and in Romans 8. On the one hand, we human beings are presented as part of the creation itself, bound into the fabric of the world, belonging to the same story as the planet, the plants, the fish and the animals. This is our created home. On the other hand, we human beings are alone 'in the image of God', transcending the rest of creation by having 'dominion' over it, like God himself. We are responsible for everything else, and not just part of it.

We meet these two complementary thoughts in Matthew 6, now modified by the good news of the kingdom of heaven. On the one hand, we are totally dependent on the earth and cannot escape our situation in it. Jesus draws this out in two ways. He reminds us of our inescapable need for food and clothing, for which we depend on

---

Text

Matthew 6:27: add a single hour to your span of life (NRSV) *or* add a foot to his height (NEB)? The confusion in translations arises from an odd combination of Greek words: a literal translation would be, which of you, by being anxious, can add one cubit [linear measure] to his age [temporal measure]? Clearly one of the words is being used metaphorically, and the other literally – but which? A complicating factor is that, just occasionally, the second is used with reference to stature: for instance, of Zacchaeus in Luke 19:3. Some long to be taller, but all of us want to live a long life, and so in all likelihood the application to age is the right one. We can extend our lives – possibly – by healthy diet and exercise, but never by worrying about it. Ultimately, God gives the tomorrow when we die (Matthew 6:34).

---

the processes of 'nature' around us. And he reminds us too that we cannot change our physical being – not just our height or age-span, but also (we may add) our particular physical constitution: we

---

Text/Theology

What does the expression 'the righteousness of God' (Matthew 6:33) mean? It seems slightly surprising, appearing alongside the kingdom of God in this important summary statement of the goal of discipleship.

Some take it to mean justice (NEB, REB), drawing out the social implications of the kingdom of God. The NRSV translation strive for . . . also points in this direction, because it turns God's kingdom and righteousness into goals which we seek to establish. But more typically God's kingdom is something which he gives, and the verb is actually seek, rather than strive for.

It could mean moral righteousness, as in Matthew 5:20 and 6:1, and possibly 5:6: the righteousness of life appropriate to the kingdom of God. This is certainly an important strand of meaning, but elsewhere it seems to mean more than just this: almost a synonym for the will of God. Thus Jesus submits to baptism by John in order to fulfil all righteousness (Matthew 3:15), and John himself comes from God in the way of righteousness (Matthew 21:32).

But why would God's will be called his righteousness? Here the Old Testament comes to our rescue. Here, quite frequently, we find God's righteousness connected with the salvation which he gives: see for instance Psalm 22:31; 23:3–4; 85:9–11. In Old Testament thinking, God's righteousness suggests the settled, peaceful life which he creates among his people when they live in fellowship and love with him and with each other, and the actions by which he brings this life into being. This is the righteousness which Jesus seeks to fulfil through his ministry (Matthew 3:15), and for which we too must seek and hunger and thirst (5:7), setting aside primary desire for all the other things which seem to offer peace and fulfilment (food, clothes, status).

cannot choose our sex or appearance, and of course many people have to come to terms with physical disabilities, sometimes very severe.

But on the other hand, Jesus tells us, we may transcend all these limitations through God our Father – not by escaping from them, but by experiencing his fatherly care and provision within them, and by striving for his 'Kingdom' and his 'righteousness'. Exercising 'dominion' over the earth in Genesis 1 has become striving for the 'Kingdom of God' in Matthew 6 – because the best possible way in which we can fulfil our appointed role, as human beings in God's image and in God's world, is by learning to accept ourselves as he has made us, to know him not just as Creator but also as Father, to trust in him to meet our daily and future needs, and to focus our ambitions ('strive') on the growth of his Kingdom, and on bringing ourselves and the world around into submission to him ('righteousness').

Concern for our environment is vital. We despise the call of God if we allow the earth to be ruined by our presence. Christians must act on behalf of the Creator to combat abuse of creation, both animate and inanimate. This is part of seeking his kingdom and righteousness. But our relationship with him as Father must lie at the heart of this seeking, enabling us to accept our particular 'lot' on the face of this planet, whatever it is.

This may be very difficult. So Paul adds a vital note of hope in Romans 8. Burdened with weakness, living in a world bound to decay, we are consumed with longing for the new creation, in which our bodies will be renewed and the world given glorious liberty.

What a vision!

The Sunday Next before Lent

Exodus 24:12–18; Psalm 2 *or* Psalm 19; 2 Peter 1:16–21;
Matthew 17:1–9

On this last Sunday before Lent we read the story of the 'Transfiguration' in all three years of the *Lectionary*. Reading it now puts us in the same position as the disciples who were with Jesus on this 'high mountain'. After this amazing revelation of his true glory, Jesus tells them that they must not mention the vision 'until after the Son of Man has been raised from the dead'. So, from one mountain, we look across the valley of Lent to the mountain of the resurrection on the other side, and remind ourselves of who Christ really is, before we descend into the valley to concentrate on his sufferings, and ours.

What does this story say about Jesus? We may summarize it in three ways:

1. He is the Son of God. This is what the heavenly voice proclaims – but the story itself reveals what this title means. The king was known as 'the son of God' in Old Testament times. In fact the heavenly words here are drawn from Psalm 2:7, where the king is addressed as the son of God. But this king shines with the glory of God himself. And Moses appears, as if to mark the parallel between this experience and his own (described in our Old Testament reading), when he too went up a mountain and entered the cloud of God's glory, to hear his voice. That glory is now focused on this person, 'my Son, the Beloved'.

2. He is the Revealer. Moses had climbed that mountain to receive the Law from God, written on stone tablets which he then carried down to the people waiting below. The disciples return down the mountain with a person, this Son of God about whom they have heard God say 'listen to him!' Moses prophesied that one day God would 'raise up for you a prophet like me from among your own people,' and added: 'you shall listen to him!' (Deuteronomy 18:15). So, subtly indicated, Jesus is introduced as the Prophet like Moses who will reveal God even more fully than Moses's stone tablets ever could.

3. He is the Servant-Saviour. Elijah also appears before the goggle-eyed disciples. Jews believed that Elijah would herald the arrival of the Messiah, as prophesied by Malachi. But the Messiah Malachi foresaw was a purifier of God's people. He would come like fire, to burn away wickedness and to refine them like impure metal. Similarly the words 'with whom I am well pleased' are drawn from Isaiah's prophecy of the coming 'Servant of the Lord' who will save God's people, ultimately by dying for them (see Malachi 3:1–4; 4:1–6; Isaiah 42:1–4; 52:13–53:12).

Theology

The authorship of 2 Peter is disputed – but whether it is by Peter or not, the passage set for today gives a very early interpretation of the transfiguration. And it is fascinating to see that it focuses only indirectly on the person of Jesus. Its primary focus is on the interpretation of prophecy. As a result of the transfiguration, we have the word of the prophets made more certain (2 Peter 1:19). This is very probably because of the allusions to Psalm 2:7 and Isaiah 42:1 in the words from heaven, quoted in 2 Peter 1:17. The experience of the glorious encounter on the mountain suddenly gives new life and meaning to the scriptures, makes powerful sense of them. The prophets, the author reminds us, were not empowered to interpret their own prophecies (v. 20), because they simply spoke as the Spirit inspired them. So now we see what the Spirit had in mind!

This sense of seeing scripture fulfilled before their very eyes deeply excited the authors of the New Testament. But this was not because they saw the Old Testament scriptures as a collection of prophecies waiting to be fulfilled, like an almanac. The two passages in mind in 2 Peter 1 illustrate how subtle their interpretation was. Psalm 2 is not a prophecy at all. It is actually about the king of Israel, reigning in Jerusalem

So, thinking of Jesus as the Servant-Saviour who purifies God's people from their sin, we enter Lent. In Lent we seek to face up to our sin, and with it the wickedness of the world around. But we carry with us the words of the Servant-Saviour to his disciples: 'Get up, and do not be afraid.'

as God's co-regent (it was probably written for a coronation ceremony). It boldly proclaims his rule as universal – extending far beyond the actual borders of the land. But in New Testament times there had been no king in Jerusalem for several hundred years. Some believed that Herod made sense of Psalm 2 and other such passages, but most rejected Herod's claim to be God's co-regent. But the early Christians became convinced that Jesus makes sense of it, because he does indeed reign universally on God's behalf – not as a literal king in Jerusalem, but spiritually. They even applied Psalm 2:7 to his resurrection (Acts 13:33). Their interpretation thus arose from their prior conviction about Jesus, but at the same time shaped and strengthened that conviction – gave it direction and force, and made them confident that God's word is indeed true.

Similarly it is not clear about whom Isaiah 42:1 is written. Who is this servant? Is it the prophet himself, or Israel, or a future messianic figure of some kind? These views were all discussed. So the field was open for the first Christians to slot Jesus into this role (quite possibly prompted by Jesus himself: see Mark 10:45). Thus they could both see him more clearly – understand something of his honour and glory, 2 Peter 1:17 – and also make sense of the scriptures as the word of God, now made more certain.

Ash Wednesday

Joel 2:1–2, 12–17 *or* Isaiah 58:1–12; Psalm 51:1–17;
2 Corinthians 5:20b–6:10; Matthew 6:1–6, 16–21 *or* John 8:1–11

We begin Lent with a sharp challenge to examine our motivation in doing 'religious' things. Jesus criticizes the hypocrites who give money, pray and practise fasting simply 'so that they may be seen and praised by others'. Does the cap fit?

Hypocrisy is a dangerous enemy, because he is a fifth column. He can infiltrate our front line, and insinuate himself into our thoughts and motivations so successfully that we hardly notice he is there. Hypocrisy works by emotional blackmail: he reminds us of our deepest needs – for affirmation, achievement and love – and slyly suggests that we can *use religion* to meet these needs. Following his lead, our religious practice becomes inward-looking, aimed at massaging our inner needs, while we *appear* to be outward-looking, focusing away from ourselves and on to Christ. Hypocrisy's final

---

Theology

Some people feel uncomfortable about the notion of 'reward' in Jesus's promise, 'your Father will reward you'. Is the Christian life a mercenary matter of seeking rewards from God? Do we only love him for our own self-advantage? We need to bear in mind that there are two sorts of reward. A hard worker is rewarded with a pay packet which recompenses her effort and achievement. But she also enjoys her job enormously, which to her is perhaps even more important a 'reward' than the pay packet. This reward is not a recompense for doing the job, but arises within the doing of it – and may in fact be the main reason for undertaking it! Ultimately, the reward our Father gives is of this second type – the reward simply of having him as Father, the reward that consists in the relationship which we seek when we shut the door and pray delightedly.

---

weapon is made of wool: if he can, he pulls it over our eyes, so that we don't even *notice* that our religious energy is chiefly directed at ourselves.

In fact a useful definition of religion, as opposed to faith, sees religion as fundamentally self-oriented, while faith is oriented on God.

Today's readings supply three tests designed to flush out hidden hypocrisy in our thoughts and motivations – three probes to test our hearts:

1. The 'secrecy' test. This is Jesus's prescription in Matthew 6. In relation to all three religious activities (giving, praying and fasting), he gives the same advice – forget the public reaction, and get alone with God. For God is 'in secret', and 'your Father who sees in secret will reward you'. In all three cases, he changes pointedly from you plural to you singular as he focuses on our *individual relationship* with God (6:2, 6,17). So the secrecy test asks: honestly, how big a

Background

Fasting was a common Jewish practice in the first century. In Matthew 6:16 the most zealous Pharisees are in mind – those who would normally fast twice a week (cf. Luke 18:12), on Mondays and Thursdays (two days after the Sabbath, and two days before). The first Christians took over the practice of fasting (see Acts 13:2–3; 14:23; 2 Corinthians 6:5; 11:27), prompted by Jesus himself (Matthew 6:17; Mark 2:19–20), although they never pursued it with as much zeal as did the Pharisees. Perhaps this is because feasting was as much a feature of the spirituality of Jesus as fasting (Mark 2:15–16; Matthew 11:19), and the first Christians of course took this over, for the Eucharist made eating together the focus of their worship. But fasting has always been an important element in Christian spirituality, especially in connection with focused or extra prayer (cf. Mark 9:29). And so it makes an excellent Lenten discipline. Why not pray rather than have lunch, once a week during Lent?

role does *privacy* (private prayer, private giving) play in your relationship with God? Suspect the presence of hypocrisy if the answer is 'Not much'.

2. The 'judgement' test. This is the test which emerges from the Old Testament reading (Joel 2). This passage is dominated by the thought of coming judgement, and the need for people to repent and to call out to God for mercy. The New Testament in no way lessens belief in the future judgement of God. So the judgement test asks: honestly, how seriously do you reckon with God's future judgement of your

---

Text

The alternative Gospel reading (John 8: 1–11) is one of the best-known Gospel stories, but is not part of the original text of John. It is only contained in one truly ancient manuscript, the fifth-century *Codex Bezae* kept in Cambridge University Library. All other chief, early manuscripts do not contain this passage. A few later manuscripts contain it, but some of these place it elsewhere – for instance after John 7:36, or after Luke 21:38, or simply attached to the end of Luke's or John's Gospel. But as time went on its position in John became more secure, and it eventually became part of the so-called Received Text of John's Gospel (the text of the majority of manuscripts, which basically became the text of the first printed edition of the Greek New Testament in 1516).

We know that many stories about Jesus and reminiscences of his teaching circulated in the early Church, and that not all of these were used by the evangelists. John himself says as much (John 21:25)! So it is by no means impossible that this story circulated at an early date. It has such intriguing qualities that it is hard to imagine it simply being invented. Jesus's attitude to the adulterous woman has a ring of authenticity about it: as does the confrontation with the religious authorities, Jesus's pointed saying in v. 7, and the extraordinary writing on the ground. Inevitably we ask what he wrote, and a simply invented story would surely supply an answer – as do some of the manuscripts: one, for instance, adds to v. 8 that Jesus wrote the sins of each of them on the ground!

---

motives and actions? Suspect the presence of hypocrisy if the answer is 'Not much'.

3. The 'sacrifice' test. Paul makes this suggestion to us in the New Testament reading (2 Corinthians 5–6). With great passion, he appeals to his readers to 'be reconciled to God', and reveals the huge sacrifices, and dedication, with which he has undertaken his ministry. We may not be called to a ministry like his, but none the less the sacrifice test asks: honestly, how much passion and readiness for sacrifice is there in your relationship with Christ? Suspect the presence of hypocrisy if the answer is 'Not much'.

Sometimes a great temptation – to adultery, fraud, wealth, adulation – can blow us apart and reveal our hearts to us in a new way, whether or not we fall into open sin. Today's Psalm (51) is traditionally associated with David's repentance after his sin with Bathsheba (2 Samuel 11–12). To discover the depths of sinful self-preoccupation in our own hearts is numbing and horrifying . . . but can be God's opportunity to create a new honesty, and awareness of himself, and discipline of character, within us – as so beautifully expressed in Psalm 51.

The First Sunday of Lent

Genesis 2:15–17; 3:1–7; Psalm 32; Romans 5:12–19;
Matthew 4:1–11

Our readings centre around the great Gospel account of the temptation of Jesus – supplemented by the Genesis story of the temptation of Adam and Eve, and by Paul's powerful picture of the parallels of light and dark between Adam and Christ in Romans 5.

The story of Jesus's temptation tells us what temptation is, in a most profound way. And when we see how Jesus's temptation replays that of Adam and Eve, we realise that all our temptations, too, will fall into one or more of these three categories. They fell, but he triumphed.

The first temptation is to doubt God's goodwill towards us. Jesus was led by God's Spirit into the desert, and is now very hungry. Has God forgotten him? The temptation is to take control, to make up for God's apparent forgetfulness or carelessness. Similarly the serpent insinuates to Eve that God's motivation was suspect, in forbidding them this fruit: he did not want them to have their eyes opened. The eminent Christian psychotherapist and spiritual director Dr Larry Crabb suggests that *doubt of God* lies at the root of the whole structure of fallenness in us: and that it must be replaced simply by *trust* in his power and love, even when he seems to have deserted us. In the end, Adam and Eve simply thought they knew better than God had said. But Jesus commits himself to trust in God's *promise* of sustenance in the wilderness.

The second temptation is to try to manipulate God to do what we want. This can be something crude (like praying for a lottery jackpot), or it can be much more subtle, like the temptation presented to Jesus. Why not do something dramatic, to express your faith and call down a wonderful demonstration of God's power? Adam and Eve felt that God could not possibly withhold from them something so obviously good and tried to pressurize God into agreeing with them, by taking the fruit. Evangelistic campaigns offering charismatic healing can fall into this trap of trying to box God into a corner so that he has to act. But wait a minute: Jesus later tells his disciples to have adventurous faith, relying on God's power: 'Heal the sick, raise the dead . . . do not take along any gold or silver, take no bag for the journey. . .' (Matthew 10:8–10). They were to rely wholly on God to care for them – just as it says in the Psalm quoted by the Devil. Where lies the difference between the Devil's temptation and Jesus's command? It lies in the very hidden area of inner motivation and direction: is our desire supremely for God's glory, or for our own? Is our prayer motivated by self-centred fear, or God-centred trust?

The third temptation is to seek our own short-cuts to God's goals. Jesus wanted to win the kingdoms of the world for God, to wrest them back out of the clutches of evil. But he cannot win them by worshipping the Devil! – even though refusing the offer means a long, hard trek to the cross and beyond. Similarly Adam and Eve saw a short-cut to wisdom, and took it. But there are no short-cuts to spiritual wisdom and maturity – just patient discipleship in the steps of the Master.

Theology

Today we begin three readings from Romans 4–5, starting with the passage which in some ways can claim to be the theological heart of the letter to the Romans. Paul's comparison between Adam and Christ contrasts their respective acts and the consequences for others. He pictures them both as inclusive figures – that is, as containing within themselves all who are related to them, so that their actions affect all their relatives. This way of thinking about Adam was common amongst Jews, as was also the belief that sin and death entered the world with Adam.

Setting Jesus on this cosmic stage illustrates his size in Paul's mind. With him, creation has been re-made, or re-started. Instead of death, life is now the future for all who are joined to Christ (this is Paul's theme in Romans 6). A process of redemption has begun which will one day embrace the whole created order, and deliver the cosmos from the slavery to decay which marks everything we see, including our own bodies (Romans 8:18–25).

The Second Sunday of Lent

Genesis 12:1–4a; Psalm 121; Romans 4:1–5, 13–17; John 3:1–17

Today's readings present us with the challenge of change – a great Lenten theme. For change is the necessary outcome of repentance, and repentance is not an act, but a lifestyle, a constant critical questioning of ourselves and our lives in the light of our growing awareness of Christ.

Abraham embraced change gladly when God called him, setting out on an adventure of faith which changed the world. Whereas later Jews praised Abraham for his obedience to God, it was his faith which fascinated St Paul, as we can see in Romans 4. Paul was strongly influenced by this story of Abraham's call in Genesis 12, where the emphasis falls on God's initiative in singling Abraham out and making dramatic promises to him. So later on, when Abraham did indeed become 'the father of many nations', this could not be described as a reward for his obedience. God had promised it, before Abraham even set out from Haran. Abraham simply responded in faith and set out into the unknown.

Nicodemus too was faced with the challenge of change. This highly respected Jewish teacher and leader heard Jesus telling him that he must be 'born again'. He must enter a whole new experience of the Spirit, allowing the Spirit to blow upon him and raise him to new life. In this picture Jesus is drawing on the famous 'Valley of Dry Bones' vision in Ezekiel 37 (set to be read in three weeks' time). Ezekiel had seen dead Israel raised to life by the wind of the Spirit. Great though his learning is, Nicodemus needs to grasp the fulfilment of this prophecy and enter 'new birth', committing himself to following Jesus and, presumably, giving up his status as 'the teacher of Israel'.

What is Nicodemus's response? We do not know how to interpret his enigmatic 'How can this be?': is it scornful, sceptical, puzzled, wistful? The challenge of change is so great that, at this point, he says no more. Later in John's Gospel he reappears, and his response is a little clearer (see John 7:50–52; 19:38–42).

Lent is a time to deepen and redirect our response to Christ: to listen again to him, study his word, pray for his Spirit, and be ready for new faith. What change or new start might he be calling us to embrace? Change is a scary prospect, and it is easy to empathize with

Abraham as he heard the call to leave his father's house. Today's Psalm (121) is designed for all who face scary journeys. In front of the traveller lie the hills, which he must cross. He does not know what dangers lurk on that lonely, distant road. But his help comes from the one who made those hills, who will watch over and keep him, preserving him from dangers both real (the sun) and imagined (the moon), until his 'going out' is completed by a 'coming in' and the journey lies joyfully behind him. That confidence can be ours also!

Theology

Paul's argument in Romans 4 seems a little abstruse to modern readers. The reason for his concentration on Abraham lies in the Jewish background to his argument. Jews looked to Abraham not just as the father of their nation, but also as their great example – the supreme Jew. In line with this he was usually portrayed as perfectly obedient to the law, even though he lived before Moses and the law had not yet been given.

Paul still treats Abraham as a supreme example of relationship with God – but he refuses to make his obedience to the law the basis of this relationship. Rather, he finds that basis in Genesis 15:6, which he quotes in Romans 4:3: Abraham believed God, and it was reckoned to him as righteousness. Righteousness means right standing before or living in harmony with God, and so Paul finds in Abraham the supreme example for gentile believers in Jesus, as well as for Jews: simply through believing God's promise, Abraham expressed and exemplified an intimate relationship with God which is now open to all who will believe in Christ, whatever their ethnic background.

The converse therefore follows: if Abraham was justified by his faith, then it could not have been on the basis of his works, his acts of obedience to the law not yet given. The verb justify (vv. 2, 5) is the verbal form of the noun righteousness (vv. 3, 5, 13), and so Paul's argument has a coherence not immediately obvious to English readers.

The Third Sunday of Lent

Exodus 17:1–7; Psalm 95; Romans 5:1–11; John 4:5–42

Our Gospel readings in Lent take us through a series of Jesus's chief encounters with individuals in John's Gospel. Last week we met Nicodemus, today the woman at the well in Samaria. There could hardly be a greater contrast between them – on the one hand the wealthy, highly respected and learned Pharisee, on the other an untouchable woman, in Nicodemus's eyes outcast by race, impure by gender, and immoral in lifestyle. Yet Jesus makes exactly the same offer to her as to him – not in terms of new birth, but of living water. He treats her with as much care and respect as him, and obtains a much more positive response than came from Nicodemus! We can trace her history through the story in four stages:

Background

The historical background of relationships between the Jews and the Samaritans brings the special dynamic of Jesus's encounter with the Samaritan woman vividly to life.

The Jews – and here we must give the term its special flavour, meaning the inhabitants of, and/or adherents of the religion of, Judea – regarded the Samaritans, who lived to the north, between Judea and Galilee, as renegades. This was ultimately because the Samaritans were held to be descended from the pagans introduced into the land by the Assyrians (2 Kings 17:24–28). But since that event in the eighth century before Christ, there had been plenty of opportunity for difference and hostility to develop. The Samaritans had their own version of the Pentateuch, and celebrated different festivals. In particular they held that Jerusalem should never have been chosen as the site for the Temple, but that it should have been built on Mount Gerizim in Samaria (the mountain to which the woman refers in John 4:20). They had different views about the Messiah, emphasizing the prophecy of

The woman is a reject, but Jesus treats her with grace. Such was the hostility between Jews and Samaritans that, if Jews had to walk through Samaria, they would normally avoid stopping. But Jesus rests beside the well at Sychar, and engages in conversation a woman who is probably an outcast even among her own people. She is amazed by his attitude, and is ready to listen to his offer of 'living water'.

The woman is a seeker, and Jesus responds with truth. Some writers regard her question about the mountain in vv. 19–20 as a religious red herring, designed to distract Jesus from the awkward topic of her sex-life. But it seems better to see her as a genuine seeker. She is not peddling the standard Samaritan line, that the Jerusalem Temple was not chosen by God, and that Mount Gerizim, rather than Mount Zion, was where all Israel should worship. She is genuinely open – ready to be critical of her own tradition. Jesus gives her a whole new explanation of worship, one which transcends all sacred places and depends on the Spirit. Those who drink the living

---

Deuteronomy 18:15 of a coming prophet like Moses (in fact in the Samaritan Pentateuch this prophecy was placed directly after the Ten Commandments).

Because the Samaritans repudiated the Jerusalem Temple, strict Jews regarded them as permanently unclean. This is the background to the comment in John 4:9, which should probably (with REB) be translated 'Jews do not share drinking vessels with Samaritans'. Jesus violates this taboo, as he asks the woman for a drink. Hostilities broke out quite frequently: the Jewish leader John Hyrcanus had destroyed the Samaritan temple on Mount Gerizim; Samaritan hotheads invaded the Jerusalem Temple and scattered cremated remains there, to make it unclean; pilgrims from Galilee on their way south to festivals in Jerusalem were not infrequently attacked or cold-shouldered (see Luke 9:52–56).

In his conversation with the woman, Jesus pointedly denies both temples a role in worship (4:21), in favour of a new worship in spirit and in truth (4:23). Dramatically, the Samaritans apparently accept this new, universalized and spiritualized worship, which requires the rejection of their own tradition, as well as that of the Jews.

water which he gives will be able to worship in Spirit and in truth.

The woman becomes a believer in Jesus as Messiah. She is ready to hear a revelation far more direct than Jesus gave to Nicodemus: 'I who speak to you am he!' (4:26). The Samaritans expected a Messiah who would chiefly be a revealer, bringing further truth to add to the Law of Moses. Jesus's knowledge of her private life impresses her that he could be the Revealer who will solve the age-old conflict with the Jews.

The woman becomes the first Christian missionary, and brings her whole town to faith in Jesus as Saviour of the world. Their confession (4:42) reveals the extent of Jesus's impact. They are ready to stop insisting on Mount Gerizim, and confess *Jesus* as the focus of world salvation. Her experience has been replayed in the lives of countless thousands since. Strangely, the vital starting-point of the story is her dreadful state of rejection and alienation – seeking acceptance and love through a series of failed relationships. On this basis she discovers the truth of the Messiah.

Read all this again – though very differently expressed – in today's magnificent Romans passage!

The Fourth Sunday of Lent

1 Samuel 16:1–13; Psalm 23; Ephesians 5:8–14; John 9:1–41

Our tour through Jesus's encounters with individuals in John's Gospel brings us to the marvellous story of the 'man born blind'. We see John's skill as a story-teller in the way the character of this stubborn, likeable man shines through.

The story is meant to illustrate the great saying at the beginning: 'As long as I am in the world, I am the light of the world' (9:5). As a sign of the truth of this claim, Jesus first restores the man's physical sight, and then – after his argument with the Pharisees – opens his spiritual eyes to see who Jesus is, and where true worship lies.

'Light' in this passage is thus a symbol for truth: particularly the truth about Jesus, the Son of Man, deserving our faith and worship. But it is more than just truth, for in his comments to the Pharisees at the end Jesus connects their false 'sight' with sin. As long as they persist in their own version of the truth, they will not be freed from sin. But – by implication – if they will follow the 'blind' man out of the synagogue, and into the worship of the Son of Man, they will be delivered from sin.

'Light' as an image for truth and for holiness – freedom from sin – is the great theme of our New Testament reading from Ephesians 5. Ephesus was a deeply pagan city. The Christians there lived in a society which tolerated dreadful abuses, including the sexual exploitation of children, widespread ritual prostitution and the permeation of occult practices and powers into every street and home. Once the Christians had been part of all this, but now they have become 'light in the Lord': doubtless Paul is referring to their conversion, marked by their baptism when they committed themselves to the rejection of pagan idolatry and occultism, and to the confession of Jesus Christ as Lord. Now, says Paul, you need to 'live as children of light', displaying your new identity by a whole new lifestyle of 'holiness and righteousness and truth'.

So they too will begin to shine. The last verse of the reading (Ephesians 5:14) is probably a quotation from an early Christian hymn, summarizing the appeal which, in effect, the Ephesian Christians make to their city: 'Wake up, O sleeper, and rise from the dead, and Christ will shine upon you!'

Doubtless their 'holiness and righteousness and truth' (5:9) were still flawed and imperfect. But Paul knew what an effect they would have, if these three colours shone brightly from their lives. Similarly the (formerly) blind man's grasp on the truth was quite slim, and yet he stuck to it unflinchingly in the face of the Pharisees' hostility. He still did not know truly who Jesus was, when he was flung out of the synagogue for loyalty to him. But he lived by the light he had.

We can be encouraged by this! It does not matter if our understanding is small. By our words and our lifestyle, we too must shine in a dark world that desperately needs the light of Christ.

Theology

The story of the blind man is told in relation to a *theological question* about the causal connection (or not) between sin and calamity. Lively faith in the reality of God's judgement on sin meant that most first-century Jews assumed that, if disaster fell, they were being punished. When Jerusalem and the Temple were destroyed by the Romans in AD 70, a vigorous debate followed: whose fault was it? – whose sin was being punished? This theology developed until some later Rabbis were prepared to make specific connections between certain illnesses and certain sins. This is a question often felt today, too: Am I being punished?

But how does a child *blind from birth* fit into such thinking? Such a child by definition could not be punished for its own sin. But according to Ezekiel 18:20, it cannot be punished for its parents' sin, either: The person who sins shall die. A child shall not suffer for the iniquity of a parent . . . Or could someone receive punishment *in advance* for sin to be committed later? Or could the birth of a handicapped child be a punishment directed at parents without compromising the truth of Ezekiel 18:20?

So the disciples, like the Pharisees, see the man born blind as a *theological problem*. (Later, the Pharisees give their answer to it: 'You were born entirely in sin – and are you trying to teach us?' (9:34). They suggest that, in his case, the whole process of conception and birth was sinful through and through. So how could his parents expect to have a healthy child?) Yet to Jesus he is not a theological problem, but a *person* in whom God's works can be revealed (9:4). He is not *acted upon* – affected by an impersonal process of cause (sin) and effect (blindness) – but potentially an *actor*, who can actually be a *revealer of God* to those around him, because of his blindness. And that is how it turns out, through this man's glorious stubbornness and refusal to be browbeaten.

Jesus does not deny the judgement of God, through this comment in 9:4. John provides us with a balancing comment in 5:14, which makes this clear. But he gives us a whole new perspective on calamity. To think of *punishment* is entirely the wrong approach. Even the most dreadful personal disasters can be occasions for *revelation of the work of God*, if we will open ourselves to his transforming power, and then unlock our lips in testimony to his love and grace.

Mothering Sunday

Exodus 2:1–10 *or* 1 Samuel 1:20–28; Psalm 34:11–20 *or*
Psalm 127:1–4; 2 Corinthians 1:3–7 *or* Colossians 3:12–17;
Luke 2:33–35 *or* John 19:25–27

Mothering Sunday services tend to be bright and breezy, with much participation by children who say and do nice things for their Mums and Grandmas. The service usually develops the theme of family life in some aspect. It can all be rather cosy and unrealistic – because mothers the world over know the true story. Motherhood is no bed of roses.

How realistic the Bible is! Here we meet motherhood in the raw. Although the two Gospel passages are strictly alternatives, it would be good to read them alongside each other. In the passage from Luke 2 Simeon warns Mary, the excited young mother, that her son will prompt great opposition, and she will feel the force of it also. His expression is so chilling – 'And you – a sword will pass through your soul also.' She must have been horrified. But never in her worst nightmares can she have imagined that, some thirty-three years later, she would stand beside a Roman cross and watch her dear Son gasp his life away in agony.

John describes the scene so simply in the second passage. It doubt-less cost Mary every ounce of strength in her body not to hurl herself against the Roman guard, shouting her Son's innocence and crying for his release. How could they sit there, calmly tearing up his clothes and casting lots for the tunic she had so lovingly woven without seams! (19:23–24). But she knew that this was his 'hour', the moment he had foreseen and had not sought to avoid. It would be disloyalty to him to protest and resist – unjust, vile, crushing though it was. So she just had to stand there, leaning on her sister and her two friends – three Marys together – and absorb the pain as the sword went through her soul.

Even in his pain Jesus knows what she is going through, and lovingly connects her with the one disciple who will be able to explain a little of what his death means, and why it had to be. Maybe the beloved disciple started by pointing out to Mary how the division of Jesus's clothes remarkably fulfilled the prophecy in Psalm 22:18, written of the suffering 'King of the Jews'.

Yes, motherhood can be agony. Moses's mother Jochebed had to choose between having her baby killed or leaving him to 'fate' in a wicker basket on the river Nile. Samuel's mother Hannah simply knew that she had to give her son up: she would keep him for a while, but as soon as he could cope she would give him away, to the God who had given him to her.

So our readings present us with three mothers who gave their children away to God – under very different circumstances, but all with pain, and with joy. The joy came through the pain, and after it. Mary knew in a unique way what Paul expresses in 2 Corinthians 1, as he writes of sharing the suffering of Christ, so that ultimately comfort may overflow from Christ to us, and through us to others also.

Application / Theology

Surrogate mothers, internet adoption, sex selection, test tube babies, post-menopausal implantation, human cloning . . . the technology of baby acquisition just keeps growing. Governments set up commissions to advise on regulating a field fraught with ethical dilemmas . . . but already we are doing things which would have shocked our grandparents. A.I.D. (artificial insemination by donor) has been available on the National Health Service for over twenty years. And at the other end of the scale, the technology of baby non-acquisition has spawned an abortion industry which terminates over 100,000 pregnancies in Britain every year.

What does the Christian view of motherhood (or of parenthood generally) have to say about all this? There is one fundamental point which is often missed because the debate focuses so quickly on more precise issues – a fundamental point which we notice clearly in today's readings: that human beings belong to God, are fundamentally his creation, have a destiny planned as a gift by him, and therefore are not at the disposal of any other. This radically affects the Christian view of parenthood. It means that we do not own our children – we have them on trust from God, and are answerable to him for our parenting of them. Remarkably, he shares with us the creating – so that our decision is part of the process: we decide to start a family, as the saying goes. But the commodity view of children – that they are got, like a new suite of furniture, or got rid of, like a grumbling appendix – is completely at odds with the Christian understanding of what, or who, they are. Baby acquisition is wrong under any circumstances, even by the normal technology of sexual intercourse!

Currently, in our culture, the ethics of personal rights so dominate the debate that this Christian view has been swamped. The right to have or not to have a baby is treated as the vital ethical principle, and the debate simply asks under what circumstances our rights should be set aside in the light of other considerations – usually the well-being of the children that might result from whatever process is being discussed. Does my right to get myself a baby outweigh the possible identity crisis that the baby will experience, when it discovers that it's not mine after all, but mothered by a surrogate or fathered by a sperm-bank?

But if we could imagine that, on all sides, everyone accepted that the commodity view of babies was wrong, and that we only ever have them on loan – then in fact the door opens to a positive evaluation of some of these new technologies. We already participate in the process to such an extent, by God's amazing grace, that these technologies are no different in principle from the technology of sexual intercourse and contraception. They are extended means of deciding how we may participate in the process of creation – a desire for which God has planted deep in our instincts. The thoughts above about children's sense of identity will, of course, feature largely as we decide – but their identity as children of God will stand, whatever process of generation they have passed through.

Inevitably, it is hard to distinguish a desire to have children from a desire to HAVE children – to possess them. But, however they come to us, that is the challenge that Christian parents face – to have our children without holding them, to have them on trust from God, knowing that their lives and destinies are his to give and theirs to discover.

The Fifth Sunday of Lent

Ezekiel 37:1–14; Psalm 130; Romans 8:6–11; John 11:1–45

Our readings gather around the theme of death – and resurrection by the Spirit of God and the power of Christ.

In the story of Lazarus we come face to face with death, in all its horror. Two sisters robbed of their brother by a sudden illness, a young man snuffed out prematurely. It sounds ordinary, because it happens all the time. But that just makes it all the more horrible. Death is a fearful enemy. How vile it is, that such ghastly things should happen so often to ordinary people in our world! We must never become immune to the pain.

Jesus himself weeps before Lazarus's grave, though he knows that, in Lazarus's case, the story will have a different ending. Does he weep for all the others who are *not* summoned back from the grave, for all the bereaved whose loss remains?

To provide a sign that reveals the glory of God through Jesus, Lazarus becomes the great exception to the universal rule. First Jesus *confronts* death with his 'I Am!' (v. 25). Then he *overthrows* death with his powerful 'Come forth!' (v. 43). Before his authority the tide of death is driven back, releasing Lazarus from its grip. In many ways, this story is the beginning of the Passion narrative in John's Gospel. Though Jesus leaves the area for a brief time (11:54), he basically remains in Jerusalem now right through to his own death and resurrection. By the way in which John introduces the story of Lazarus, it is clear that Jesus returns to Bethany, to help the family he loves, only at the cost of his own life. Opposition to Jesus in Jerusalem has become so strong that the disciples try to stop him from going (v. 8), and Thomas gruffly remarks, 'Let us also go, that we may die with him!' (v. 16).

Thomas says far more than he is aware of. To die with Jesus: that is the secret of resurrection. Jesus puts his own head into the noose, in order to save Lazarus, but from another angle he can only save Lazarus by becoming the Resurrection as well as the Life. He will die, so that he can absorb Lazarus's death into himself, and thus convey to him the power of his own resurrection.

That is the secret that Paul expresses so vividly in Romans 8. 'If Christ is in you,' he says, then his resurrection power will bring us to life also through the indwelling Holy Spirit.

And Ezekiel too said far more than he was aware of. His 'valley of dry bones' vision was a picture of return from exile: God would bring his people back and re-establish them in the promised land. It would be like resurrection from the dead. But John reminds us of Ezekiel's vision as he shows Jesus opening Lazarus's grave and bringing him out (see Ezekiel 37:12). Through Jesus, God will do something far more wonderful for his people than just political restoration. He will conquer death for them!

And so, as Passiontide begins, our thoughts turn to the end of the story, the glorious outcome for all who face the agony of death with Christ beside them.

Theology

Two things are remarkable about St Paul's view of the Holy Spirit, both of them visible in Romans 8:6–11, our New Testament reading. The first is that he calls him the Spirit of Christ, and suggests that if the Spirit indwells us then Christ is in us (8:10), since – like all Jews – he believed that the Spirit was fundamentally *God*'s Spirit, possessed by him just as the human spirit inhabits each person (1 Corinthians 2:11). This sharing of ownership of the Spirit between God and Christ is a truly remarkable step for a monotheistic Jew to take – and speaks volumes about the *instinctive* position that Paul, in common with the other New Testament writers, gave to Jesus.

The second remarkable feature is the connection Paul makes between the Spirit of Christ and our mortal bodies

(Romans 8:11). For Paul, the Spirit does not inhabit a spiritual bit of us: it inhabits our bodies, because our bodies are essential to our identity, and not just an incidental addition to the real us. In the biblical tradition generally, we do not have a body, but we *are* a body (and a mind, and a heart, and a spirit). And for Paul the *bodily* residence of the Holy Spirit is the basis of his resurrection hope. What this means is that the intimate relationship which we have with Christ now, by his Spirit, will transcend our physical death, and carry us through into a new giving of life to our mortal bodies. Paul expresses it so beautifully later in Romans 14: If we live, we live to the Lord; and if we die, we die to the Lord. So then, whether we live or whether we die, we are the Lord's (Romans 14:8).

It is right to anticipate this resurrection hope during Lent. For otherwise the pain of present weakness would be unbearable.

Palm Sunday

Liturgy of the Palms

Matthew 21:1–11; Psalm 118:1–2, 19–29

This 'very large crowd', who greeted Jesus so enthusiastically, had definite ideas about why he had come to Jerusalem. 'Son of David' (v. 9) and 'prophet' (v. 11) were titles loaded with political significance. It looked as though he might at last lead a successful revolution against the Romans, and throw them out of the holy city. Their messianic fervour quickly evaporated when they realised that this was not his agenda.

Maybe they began to get the message (if they were thoughtful) when they saw him riding the donkey. Clearly Jesus acted deliberately to fulfil Zechariah's prophecy (Zechariah 9:9), as Matthew points out. Any who spotted the significance of his action will also have known how that prophecy continues: 'He will cut off

---

Text / Background

The waving of palm branches, associated with Palm Sunday, is not mentioned in Matthew's or Mark's version of the story. In Matthew the crowd cuts branches from trees, and strews these on the road. In Mark, it is foliage gathered from the fields (Mark 11:8). No waving goes on, in either. The palm branches come from John's version, where we read that the festival crowd, hearing that Jesus was approaching Jerusalem, took palm branches and came out to meet him, shouting Hosanna . . . (John 12:13).

Older commentators reconstructed the scene as follows: one crowd accompanies Jesus on the last stage of his journey, and witnesses his action in stopping to obtain and mount the donkey. Another crowd comes out to meet him, waving palm branches. The two crowds meet, and then one group goes before and the other follows (Matthew 21:9) as Jesus moves down the Mount of Olives towards the city.

---

the chariot from Ephraim, and the war horse from Jerusalem . . . and he shall command peace to the nations' (Zechariah 9:10).

So Jesus goes immediately into the Temple, to confront the corruption of prayer, rather than to the Roman fortress, to confront unwanted government. Our Lord Jesus Christ is the Prince of Peace, and his name can never rightly be used to sanction political violence. Wherever it is so used – in the Crusades, in pogroms against the Jews, in Beirut and Indonesia and Northern Ireland today – then his name ends up in the dust along with the victims.

John's mention of palm branches gives the celebration a particular symbolism. It not only reminds us of the celebrations surrounding the restoration of the Temple in 164 BC (2 Maccabees 10:7) and the victorious entry of Simon Maccabaeus into Jerusalem in 141 BC (1 Maccabees 13:51), but also – more particularly – of the regular celebrations at the Feast of Tabernacles, when the waving of palm branches was a sign of great rejoicing and thanksgiving (see 2 Maccabees 10:6). Passover and Tabernacles are combined when Jesus arrives.

John, on the other hand, does not mention the throwing of cloaks and coats on to the road (Matthew 21:8; Mark 11:8). This seems to have symbolized the recognition and acclamation of kingship by the crowd – see the background in 2 Kings 9:13. This is also the significance of calling Jesus Son of David, which likewise appears just in Matthew and Mark.

Palm Sunday

Liturgy of the Passion

Isaiah 50:4–9a; Psalm 31:9–16; Philippians 2:5–11;
Matthew 26:14–27:66 *or* Matthew27:11–54

Matthew's long Passion Narrative is dominated by Jesus's words in 26:53–56. What happens to him is dreadfully unjust, but events are driven not by his enemies, but by something deeply mysterious, the fulfilment of the scriptures. Behind the betrayal, the fear, the hatred and the degradation there works the hidden purpose of God, to which Jesus deliberately conforms – and Matthew wants to make it clear.

Ironically, immediately after his words in 26:55–56, Jesus's disciples turn tail and flee, thus fulfilling Zechariah 13:7 as Jesus had said they would (26:31). At his trial before Caiaphas Jesus quotes Psalm 110:1 and Daniel 7:13, claiming that they are about to be

Background

We cannot be certain that Philippians 2:6–11 is an early hymn which existed prior to Paul's letter, but this is the view of most experts. Most modern translations, like JB, NIV, and NRSV (but not REB), print it with indented lines to make clear that it appears to be a poetic insert in celebration of Jesus.

Two pieces of evidence combine to support this suggestion: **(1) Language** – we meet several unusual words here, not typical of Paul, and the passage contains short, weighty phrases typical of Hebrew poetry. **(2) Ideas** – though the section fits into Philippians beautifully, relating powerfully to Paul's leading thoughts in this letter, it none the less contains unusual ideas, like that of Jesus's self-emptying (v. 7), the strange phrase he did not count equality with God something to be grasped (either grabbed for or held on to (v. 6), and the notion of Jesus's obedience unto death (v. 8).

fulfilled (26:64). Then Judas regrets betraying Jesus and throws the thirty pieces of silver down in the Temple, thus symbolically repeating the action of Zechariah by which he had proclaimed the end of the covenant with Judah and Israel (Zechariah 11:12–14; Matthew 27:3–10). Pilate, by washing his hands in public (27:24), unconsciously enacts the ritual by which the guilt of innocent blood could be averted from the people (Deuteronomy 21:1–8). This is highly ironic, in view of the words of the people in 27:25.

Then, through a series of details in the story, Matthew shows how Psalm 22 was fulfilled by different people: by the soldiers who mocked him and divided his clothes (27:29, 35; Psalm 22:7, 18), by the passers-by who shook their heads (27:39; Psalm 22:7), by the authorities who mocked him (27:42), unconsciously echoing the words of Psalm 22:8, and by Jesus himself, who echoes Psalm 22.1 in his cry from the cross (27:46).

When we add the fulfilment of Psalm 69:21 in 27:48, and of Daniel 12:2 in 27:52, we realise how powerfully Matthew has made his point. God is working his purpose out, hidden in the horrors of this vile event, steering it towards his goal, which is life, not death.

Experts have pored over this text, trying to extract the last ounce of meaning from it. Is Jesus being pictured like Adam here – in the form /image of God? Or like Isaiah's suffering servant, as in today's Old Testament reading, which gives us one of Isaiah's four servant songs? Does Jesus start equal with God, give it up and then return to that position, or does he start less than equal with God, only to be given that honour when every tongue confesses him Lord (v. 11, the name of God in the Old Testament)? What are the beings in heaven and under the earth who will submit to him – and what kind of prospect is this? And how did it come about that, at such an early date, Christians were applying to Jesus texts like Isaiah 45:23, which reappears here in vv. 10–11 and which in Isaiah is clearly applied to God himself?

These are fascinating questions. But it would be all too possible to get caught up in thinking about this hymn rather than singing it, which is surely what St Paul would want us to do.

This might seem to alienate the story of the Passion from our experience. Who can claim, like Jesus, to have scripture fulfilled through his or her sufferings? Don't we have to suffer without that kind of comfort? But Paul helps us with this, in the New Testament reading from Philippians. He encourages us to 'let the same mind be in you that was in Christ Jesus' (Philippians 2:5; NRSV), and then quotes a glorious early hymn celebrating the self-giving and exaltation of Jesus – his incarnation, death and resurrection. Paul wants the Philippians to think of their own sufferings with the same mind as Jesus: and the background to this is his comment at the end of the previous chapter, that God has graciously granted you the privilege not only of believing in Christ, but of suffering for him as well (Philippians 1:29; NRSV). In other words, *their* sufferings come to them within the will of God for them just as much as the sufferings of Jesus himself – and with the same goal in view, that they too, like him, should go via the cross to the resurrection (see especially Philippians 3:10–11).

The Monday of Holy Week

Isaiah 42:1–9; Psalm 36:5–11; Hebrews 9:11–15; John 12:1–11

During Holy Week the lectionary takes us through the four so-called 'Servant Songs' in Isaiah, reaching a climax with the fourth and most famous, Isaiah 53, on Good Friday. The identity of 'the servant' in Isaiah is mysterious. On the one hand Israel, the nation, is called 'my servant' in 49:3, but on the other hand we discover only two verses later that 'the servant' has a divine commission to save Israel (49:5–6). It is not surprising that the first Christians found a prophecy of Jesus in these passages, and we follow in their steps this week. Today, the first song celebrates the Servant's universal ministry of gentle justice.

Similarly the New Testament readings in Holy Week form a series, reflecting on the death of Christ from different angles:

Monday: Hebrews 9:11–15, Jesus's death as the perfect sacrifice for sin.

Tuesday: 1 Corinthians 1:18–31, Jesus's death as foolishness, as the reversal of the world's values.

Wednesday: Hebrews 12:1–3, Jesus's death as example for us.

Maundy Thursday: 1 Corinthians 11:23–26: Jesus's death in eucharistic representation.

Friday: Hebrews 10:16–25 *or* 4:14–16; 5:7–9: Jesus's death as the basis of access to God.

And the Gospel readings also form a series. Today we begin four readings from John 12 and 13, chapters in which John prepares his readers for the approaching death of Jesus. Each passage introduces us to a different aspect of the Passion. This first episode, the story of the dinner in Bethany at which Mary anoints Jesus's feet with pure nard, looks forward to the last episode in John 19:38–42, where Joseph and Nicodemus anoint Jesus's body with myrrh and aloes for burial. She uses one litre, they use one hundred. But Jesus himself makes the connection clear: 'She has kept it to use for the day of my burial.' The 'nard' she uses was very expensive aromatic ointment, imported from northern India, and used particularly for anointing the dead. So Mary knows what she is doing, as she worships at Jesus's feet and fills the house with the fragrance of her love:

Her worship is heart-felt, unlike that of Judas, who pays lip-service to their public devotion to the poor. With the nard, she pours out all the love of her heart to this Jesus who came back, at the cost of his own life, to save her brother.

Her worship is costly. She symbolizes the depth of her love by giving him the most precious and significant thing she possesses. Judas objects to the extravagance. But true love for Christ will always be extravagant.

Her worship is open-eyed to the death of Christ. She knows that Jesus is about to die. Unlike the twelve disciples, she realises that her love and worship must embrace his death and departure, and not shy away from it. All true worship is centred upon the death of Christ, embracing his pain and suffering, making it the heart of our faith, celebrating it as the foundation of our salvation.

As the author to the Hebrews puts it in our New Testament reading, it is the blood of Christ by which we are cleansed, 'so that we may serve the living God'. Christianity cannot be turned into a collection of bright philosophical ideas, for at its heart is the worship of a dying man, Jesus Christ our Saviour, who by his death transforms our death into life – just as he did for Lazarus.

Holy Week thus begins with an invitation to share the worship of Mary, bowing at Jesus's feet in sorrow and adoration.

The Tuesday of Holy Week

Isaiah 49:1–7; Psalm 71:1–14; 1 Corinthians 1:18–31;
John 12:20–36

The second 'Servant song', from Isaiah 49, describes the double task of the Servant. The 'islands' and 'distant nations' (v.1; NIV) are introduced to one for whom it is too small a thing to be the Saviour just of Israel: he is also to be 'a light for the Gentiles, that you may bring my salvation to the ends of the earth' (v. 6). In due time, though the Servant will be despised and abhorred, yet kings and princes will see and bow down (v. 7). Isaiah had a powerful, world-wide vision of God's purposes.

The New Testament, of course, sees Jesus as this 'Servant'. And the thought of his world-wide mission often appears, even when this title is not used. In 1 Corinthians 1:18–31 Paul presents Jesus as 'the wisdom of God' for Jews and 'Greeks' alike – 'Greeks' representing the whole non-Jewish world. All other human ideas of 'wisdom' are made 'foolish' by the wisdom of God displayed in Christ crucified. A crucified wretch, a figure of shame and degradation – how could such an eyesore be the centre of God's world plan? Jews and 'Greeks' shared the horrified reaction to such an idea. But he is not only God's wisdom, says Paul, but our 'righteousness, holiness and redemption' (v. 30). It is God's way, to choose the weak and wretched in order to 'shame' the strong (v. 27).

This is the message also of our Gospel reading, the second instalment from John's introduction to the Passion. Two Greeks approach Jesus's disciples, asking for an interview with Jesus. Strangely, Jesus does not agree to see them. The time for talking is past. In any case, what he has to offer them is not the kind of 'wise talk' for which, as Greeks, they are looking. They approach him as a teacher and philosopher, but he offers them his death, which he pictures as the moment of his glorification. He plays on the double meaning of the word 'lift up' – both 'raise' and 'exalt' – as he says, 'I, when I am lifted up from the earth, will draw all people to myself' (12:32; NRSV). His coming crucifixion will be seen as the explosion of his messianic claim by many. How can such a pathetic, rejected figure be the Christ of God? But on the contrary, says Jesus, this rejection will be the moment of glorification, of being 'lifted up', so that people all over the world, including these 'Greeks', will be drawn to him.

Paul faced the unlikeliness of this as he experienced the rejection of his message by Jews and 'Greeks' who could not accept a crucified Saviour. But his words in 1 Corinthians 1 will be more than vindicated this Easter, as hundreds of millions of Christians world-wide will gather to worship 'Christ crucified'. We lightly domesticate the symbol of the cross, evacuate it of its horror, and lose the sense of exultation with which Paul proclaimed this sign of weakness and shame as the heart of God's good news. We hang it around our necks, inscribe it on our graves, bishops incorporate it into their signatures, we even shape it neon and put it over our churches. But it is still horrible: a sign of torture and agony. But what hope it brings! It enables us to say to today's Greeks: Forget the adverts – forget the

Background

The Messiah remains for ever . . . and who is this Son of Man? The question of the crowd in John 12:34 is a little puzzling. Their reference to the law is probably quite specific: Psalm 89:37 says that the line of the Davidic king shall continue for ever, and his throne endure like the sun. Texts like this were transferred to the coming Messiah (who was called the son of David), when the Davidic line failed. Messianic beliefs amongst Jews varied considerably, and in one tradition the Messiah was expected to reign for a period, and then die (4 Ezra 7:28–29). But the general belief was that the messianic kingdom would endure for ever on earth, once the Messiah came.

John does not picture this crowd as hostile towards Jesus, but as listening carefully and taking seriously his messianic claim. But that is what puzzles them. He is clearly talking about his own death: so how is this compatible with claiming to be Messiah?

Interestingly they also see that Jesus is calling himself the Son of Man (putting vv. 23 and 32 together), and realise that 'Son of Man' must be a name for the Messiah. But they are puzzled by this name. What does it mean? Jesus frequently used this name of himself (although scholars have disputed how many of the appear-success culture that leaves you a failure – forget the cult of youth and beauty that makes your handicap a vile blemish – forget your wretched past with all its sins and regrets – forget your fear of death, and of dying: *God* made himself abhorrent for you, became a reject, a joke, a criminal, and died a ghastly death for you, so that he might absorb your sin, pain and death into himself, and bring you into light, and life!

---

ances of the term on Jesus's lips actually go back to him). Unlike 'son of David', the expression had no clear association with the Messiah, as its use in the Old Testament makes clear: Ezekiel the prophet is often addressed by God as son of man, emphasizing his frailty and humanity, and Daniel sees one like a son of man approaching God to receive power, authority and kingdom in Daniel 7:13–14. But this vision is very obscure in meaning. We could ask about Daniel 7:13–14 the same question as the crowd: who is this son of man?

It looks as though Jesus used the title precisely because of its obscurity and allusiveness. If people were reminded of Daniel 7, they would see the connection with Jesus's proclamation of the kingdom of God. But they would still be left wondering *what sort of* kingdom this son of man was receiving, and bringing. And here in John 12 we see the same puzzlement: v. 23 suggests that the moment for the fulfilment of the vision of Daniel 7 has come – *now* the son of man will receive the glory! But this lifting up (v. 32) is clearly also going to be his *death* (his literal lifting up on to the cross). How can his *death* be the moment of his glory?

Jesus does not explain in detail, but urges them to keep following him (vv. 35–36)!

The Wednesday of Holy Week

Isaiah 50:4–9a; Psalm 70; Hebrews 12:1–3; John 13:21–32

The third Servant Song, which we read today, imagines the words of the Servant himself as he faces something so surprising and unexpected – rejection by the people he has come to save. He comes ready to 'sustain the weary' with the message he has heard from God (v. 4), but instead finds himself beaten, humiliated and mocked (v. 6). Yet he is not deflected from his determination ('I have set my face like flint'), and casts himself upon God who will help and vindicate him. With 'the Sovereign Lord' beside him, no human condemnation will be final. Today's Psalm movingly expresses the same faith in the face of rejection and hostility.

And in just this way, in our Gospel reading, Jesus comes face to face with the horror of rejection – by one of his own disciples. John describes the incident carefully. He makes clear first that the disciples

Background

Hebrews 12:1–3, our New Testament reading, develops the same theme of the hostility shown towards Jesus. And in describing his reaction to this hostility, the author uses a powerful metaphor from athletics. The metaphor comes alive when we imagine the kind of stadium in which Greek games were held – for instance the stadium at Delphi, which is not circular but long, with rows of banked seating on either side of a straight track. The athletes, who ran naked (laying aside every weight!) raced from the end down one side towards a marker at the other end, rounded it sharply and ran back down the other side to the finish. Thus they always ran with a goal visible in front of them – the half-way marker, or the finishing line. And the cloud of witnesses surrounded them closely, with the seats close to the track on either side.

The author of Hebrews encourages his readers to run the Christian life like this, with their eyes focused on the goal which is

78

were completely taken aback by Jesus's revelation that one of them would betray him, and then that Jesus identifies Judas privately just to 'the beloved disciple' who is reclining next to him. Actually, Jesus first mentions in John 6:70 his awareness that one of his disciples is 'a devil', and John comments there that Jesus 'had known from the beginning which of them did not believe and who would betray him' (6:64). So all through his ministry he has carried the private agony that one of his inner circle, who looks as devoted as all the rest, is not a true believer and will one day turn against him.

Now the moment has come, and Jesus watches helplessly as Judas leaves the circle to betray him. He still *looks* like a devoted disciple (vv. 28–29), but there is treachery in his heart (see also 13:2).Jesus says nothing, and lets him go, so that the word of God may be fulfilled (v. 18) – the word in Psalm 41:9 which, like Isaiah 50, hinted at the rejection of the Messiah.

In Matthew and Mark, the disciples greet Jesus's announcement with the sad question, 'Surely not I, Lord?' They do not want to betray Jesus, but they know that a great test of loyalty is coming.

Jesus. He is at the finishing line because he has run the race before them, and his example thus inspires them in their struggle. He kept his eye fixed on the joy to come, after the shame of the cross.

The word shame is evocative. The author moves from a metaphor in which nakedness was socially acceptable (for athletes at the games) to a horrible reality in which nakedness symbolized total degradation and shame. Jesus was not crucified with a neat loin-cloth, but naked. That was just one aspect of the shame endured by all who were crucified. It meant the total loss of all status, recognition and social worth, not to mention the awful physical agony. But Jesus despised the shame – i.e. he treated the shame as shameful, as worthy of disgrace, he did not submit to it – because he saw joy approaching at God's right hand. Look to him, says the author to his readers, who were experiencing social shame because of their faith: he is the beginner and finisher of our faith: he started the race, and finished it!

Clearly, one of them is going to 'crack'. Which will it be? In the event, they all betray him simply by deserting him in his hour of need. The Servant must stand alone before his accusers, trusting only in God to vindicate him.

Here in John, this thought of vindication is expressed most remarkably by Jesus's words as Judas leaves: 'Now is the Son of Man glorified, and God is glorified in him!' (v. 31). Because he fulfils the role of the rejected Servant of the Lord, his betrayal is actually a moment of *glory* for him. This is such an extraordinary thought that it is hard to take in. But John will reinforce it later, by picturing Jesus's crucifixion – amazingly – as *an enthronement*. The rejection of Jesus was not a glorious action, but a dreadful deed turned into a glorious fulfilment of God's plan of salvation.

Judas's betrayal was premeditated, but the other disciples were simply pressurized by fear. In what ways do we betray him still, by our absence, or our silence, or our pretence? Or maybe our need at the moment is not to ask in what way we may be like Judas, but to compare ourselves with *Jesus*. At some point we all feel the pain of betrayal by friends or family. In such experiences, he stands alongside us, and points us towards *quiet faith in God's vindication*. He has been there before us.

Maundy Thursday

Exodus 12:1–4, 11–14 *or* 1–14; Psalm 116:1–2, 12–19;
1 Corinthians 11:23–26; John 13:1–17, 31b–35

Today we remember Our Lord's Last Supper with his disciples, on the eve of his crucifixion, and his institution of the Eucharist. The Gospels consistently describe the Last Supper as a Passover meal, celebrated in line with the instructions in Exodus 12, although according to John it took place a day earlier than the normal Passover celebration. Today's Psalm is one of the so-called *Hallel* Psalms (113–118) which were sung at the Passover meal.

Another fascinating difference between John and the other Gospels is that, while the others recount Jesus's adaptation of the Passover meal, changing it into a memorial of himself rather than of the Exodus from Egypt, John does not mention this at all, but instead tells the story of the feet-washing by Jesus. Probably there is no intended contradiction between the Gospels here. In fact they dovetail with each other, for Luke records that, during the meal, a dispute arose among the disciples as to which of them was the greatest. In response Jesus told them that the greatest is the one who serves, and that 'I am among you as one who serves' (Luke 22:24–27). Jesus's words in Luke would come home with great force, if at the same time he washed his disciples' feet as described by John.

And further, *John's* emphasis – on Jesus's example of self-giving service – coincides precisely with *Paul's* in 1 Corinthians 11. Paul's concern, in reminding the Corinthians of the institution of the Eucharist, is not historical. He tells them roundly that, at the moment when you come together, it is not really to eat the Lord's supper (11:20) – because they are not caring for each other, and their *divisions* are obvious (11:18, 21). How can they celebrate one who gave himself for you (11:24), when they so pointedly don't do that for each other?

Our Gospel story makes two points, very powerfully. Firstly, all who want to be associated with Jesus must submit to ministry from him. This seems a simple point, but it has hidden depths. Peter is horrified at the idea of Jesus washing his feet, and refuses. His pride and embarrassment dress themselves up as concern for Jesus's dignity. He wants to keep Jesus in the 'Lord and Teacher' category (see v. 13), for he is comfortable with that. He knows where he stands. For us, too, it is much easier to recite the Creed, naming Jesus as 'Lord', 'Son of God', 'true God from true God', and 'one in being with the Father', than actually, personally and deeply to admit our need of 'cleansing'. We may kneel at the altar-rail, but the symbolism of that is wrong. *He kneels before us,* too, offering us cleansing from our sin, restoration from our pride, and forgiveness for our neglect and lack of love. But we cannot receive this unless we are prepared to admit, unreservedly, that we are sinful, proud and unloving.

Secondly, this story presents Jesus as an example to follow. 'You

Background

Experts have argued long and hard about whether the Last Supper was a Passover meal or not. It is presented as such in the synoptic Gospels (e.g. Matthew 26:17ff), but in John Jesus is actually crucified on the day of preparation for the Passover (John 19:14), and so the meal in John 13 cannot have been a Passover meal unless it happened a day early.

This strange problem over timing is actually helpful for our understanding of the relationship between Last Supper and Passover. It is hard to set aside the strong Gospel tradition that it was a Passover meal: but if it was celebrated a day early, then that is simply the first of several changes that Jesus introduced, all of which must have taken the disciples by surprise. In all likelihood they had eaten Passover together in other years, but never before had Jesus:

– said such a strange thing when breaking the unleavened bread ('This is my body, which is given for you').
– said such a strange thing over the third cup of the meal, the so-called cup of blessing (cf. 1 Corinthians 10:16) – 'This cup is the new covenant in my blood' – and then refrained from drinking it himself. (He may even have broken with usual practice and passed round his own cup for them to drink, rather than filling a separate cup for each.)

must do the same!', he tells his disciples, and then elaborates this in terms of love for one another. Love will be their badge of membership, marking them as his disciples (v. 35). This too cuts deep through our pretensions and self-deceptions. Behind all their activity and apparent success, our churches are often riven by factionalism and stifled by dead formalism. We fight for our corner, and worship becomes an arena for competition, not a hospital for sick souls.

As we celebrate the one who gave his body and blood for us, let us seek grace again to give ourselves for one another, as he did.

- cut short the meal, abandoning the final cup of consummation – saying that he would not drink of the fruit of the vine again until he drank it new in God's kingdom.
- so pointedly re-directed the memorial away from the Exodus and on to himself – do this in remembrance (not of the Exodus, but) of me!
- celebrated the Passover without a lamb. (This last point is not certain – but if the meal was held early it would have been difficult to acquire a lamb, and the new symbolism given by Jesus to the unleavened bread would have been powerfully strengthened, if their meal did not have a proper Passover lamb.)

It was a real Passover meal, but Jesus hijacked it, knowing what lay ahead, and performed actions which re-wrote the disciples' sense of who they were. Previously, their celebration of Passover had confirmed their identity as Jews, as they looked back to the unique events which had shaped Israel as a nation. But now – apparently – they must focus their memorial on the death of Jesus as an identity-giving event of greater significance even than the Exodus.

Hence the vital significance of the Eucharist to Christians: it defines, expresses and strengthens our identity as the people of Jesus the Christ, living in fellowship with him and with each other.

Good Friday

Isaiah 52:13–53:12; Psalm 22; Hebrews 10:16–25 *or*
Hebrews 4:14–16; 5:7–9; John 18:1–19:42

The Servant Songs build towards a climax. From the first three, we would never suspect what we meet in the fourth. We have heard that the Servant will care for the weak (42:1–4), and bring world-wide salvation (49:1–6) while being himself rejected (50:4–9). But now we find that his rejection will mean his *death,* and that this death will be 'for' others. As a sacrifice, he will bear our sin, so that we can be healed. And his death will not be the end: 'he will see his offspring and prolong his days . . . after the suffering of his soul, he will see light and be satisfied' (vv. 10–11). This is how he will care for the weak, and bring salvation to the world.

Remarkably, details of this vision apply directly to Jesus, who quite literally was 'assigned a grave with the wicked, and with a rich man in his death' (Isaiah 53:9): John, like the other Gospels, tells of Jesus's crucifixion with two criminals, and his burial by wealthy Joseph of Arimathea.

We need *dramatic pictures* to discover the meaning of Jesus's death. In Hebrews 10 the author draws on the Gospel incident of the rending of the Temple veil (see Matthew 27:51) to express the thought that, through the tearing of Jesus's body, we have been given access into the 'Most Holy Place' where God is. The 'Most Holy Place' was the inner area of the Temple before which the veil hung, and was out of bounds to all except the High Priest, who entered it once a year, on the Day of Atonement. The rending of this veil signals *open access* to God – and the author of Hebrews simply links the veil and the body of Jesus: they were both *torn,* so that we might march boldly into the presence of God.

Similarly, in Hebrews 4:14–16 and 5:7–9, we have to imagine trembling with fear as we enter a throne room, bringing a plea to a king. Oriental kings are notoriously aloof, and abrupt with the frailties of their subjects. But we find – amazingly – that *this King couldn't sympathize more,* because he stepped into the life of one of his own subjects, and experienced all its pain and frustration himself. The author draws on the story of Jesus's agony in Gethsemane (Matthew 26:36–46) to underline the extent of Jesus's sympathy and self-offering.

These thoughts supplement John's powerful Passion Narrative, which we read today. John is silent about the agony in Gethsemane, for his interest lies not in emphasizing Jesus's pain, but in drawing out other aspects of the story:

1. *Jesus's voluntary submission to death.* John emphasizes Jesus's *control* over his own arrest by the temple guard (18:1–11)! Similarly, when Pilate asserts his power over Jesus, he replies, 'You would have no power over me, if it were not given to you from above' (19:11), and this is ironically confirmed when Pilate tries to release Jesus and cannot (19:12)! It is not God's will for him to be released.

2. *The injustice of Jesus's condemnation.* He is condemned to die after a mockery of justice, during which his request for witnesses is denied (18:21–22). The Jews refuse to bring a specific charge (18:29–30), and Pilate flogs Jesus and hands him over for crucifixion even though he repeatedly says that he finds no basis for any charge (18:38; 19:6). In John, no trial of Jesus in fact takes place.

3. *The apostasy of the Jews.* The Jews claim loyalty to the Law in opposing Jesus (19:7), and refuse to enter the Antonia Fortress, Pilate's headquarters, to avoid defilement at Passover (18:28). But their condemnation of Jesus ironically leads them to a total repudiation of their own Passover confession of faith: we have no king but the emperor! (19:15). In line with his message throughout the Gospel, John is making the point that only faith in Jesus makes sense of the Law, the Old Testament scriptures.

4. *The King on the cross.* Ironically, Pilate almost ends up confessing faith in Jesus. Here is your King! he says, as he presents Jesus to the Jews (19:14), and he refuses to alter the inscription on the cross (19:22). Ironically, 19:13 could be translated, 'Pilate made Jesus sit on the judges' bench', and undoubtedly John intended this double meaning. Through all this rejection and injustice, Jesus is being glorified (12:23; 13:31), and in a real sense he is *enthroned* on the cross (19:19–22) as he is 'lifted up' for all to see and believe in (3:14–15; 12:32).

5. *The Passover Lamb.* Jewish readers, following the chronology of John's account (especially 19:14), would be aware that Jesus died at

the very time when the lambs were being sacrificed in the Temple for the Passover meal that evening. John draws this out explicitly by quoting a verse about the Passover lamb in 19:36. This Jesus truly is 'the lamb of God, who takes away the sin of the world' (John 1:29)!

Easter Eve

Job 14:1–14 *or* Lamentations 3:1–9, 19–24; Psalm 31:1–4, 15–16;
1 Peter 4:1–8; Matthew 27:57–66 *or* John 19:38–42

We watch, and wait, while Jesus rests in the tomb. Easter Eve is a
time to share the agony of grief and disappointment felt by the
disciples on that Passover Sabbath. We share it, not because we pretend that we do not know what happens next, but because the agony
of standing beside a grave is felt daily by so many in our world.
Mothers, children, husbands and wives – what can soften the pain of
sheer loss as they stand and grieve? On Easter Eve we grieve too: for
all the premature deaths, the casualties of injustice, the victims of
war and terror, the starved children and neglected poor, the vast collective cry that rises to God from the tortured earth of our world,
crying like the blood of Abel for justice and release.

On Easter Eve there is no obvious hope. The grave is closed, the
guard has been set. Don't let those deceivers try to steal the body,
and pretend that there is anything but a final end, a termination of
light and hope. The Christ is gone, aspiration is dead. All we have is
a memory of a temporary, illusory joy.

If mortals die, will they live again? cries Job (14:14). He lives with
a terrible sense of *incompleteness:* the story of his life will be cut
short, if he dies without vindication. Is there no answer, is there
nothing more than dust, no Voice to give reason to his existence? He
longs for God to 'appoint me a set time, and remember me' (14:13;
NRSV) – for there to be a *moment* when his life makes sense before
the God whose *inscrutability* seems to make a nonsense of everything.

At moments of greatest pain, God is silent. Though I call and cry
for help, he shuts out my prayer (Lamentations 3:8). And yet the very
act of *voicing our agony to him* causes faith to rise. I have hope! The
steadfast love of the LORD never ceases (Lamentations 3:22). How
did the disciples talk to each other, and to God, on Easter Eve? Were
there moments of glad trust in God, even though they were left without explanation or assurance, feeling the full horror of their grief,
and expecting at any moment to be arrested and executed as the followers of this now exposed 'Messiah'?

The fact is that 'Easter Eve' is the normal state of God's world.

Tomorrow we will rejoice in what Paul calls 'the *hope* of the resurrection' (Acts 23:6): though we believe that Jesus actually rose from the dead, resurrection is not yet a fact of our experience. We know all about death. But not yet about victory over it.

Easter Eve is where we live. So it is a time for togetherness, a time to hold on to each other in love, to comfort each other, to speak of the Lord, to remember his words, to renew our love for those whom we have lost in death, and to look forward with hope and longing to the victory and the justice yet to be. And to remember that we are not alone in our grief. A Father stands with us, beside the grave of his Son.

Background / Theology

Why did Easter Eve occur? The first Christians must have asked, Why did our Lord not rise, victoriously, as soon as his death had been clearly confirmed? Peter gives one small answer in our New Testament reading: during this period Jesus went and preached to 'the dead', in the hope that they too might 'live in spirit' (1 Peter 4:6). It is unclear who exactly are the dead here, but probably Peter is thinking of the 'spirits in prison' to whom he describes Jesus preaching, during this period between his death and resurrection, in 1 Peter 3:19–20. These were the half-human, half-angelic beings who led the rebellion against God in the period before the Flood (see Genesis 6:2–4). They were not destroyed in the Flood, so tradition held, but kept in a spiritual prison for later judgement. Jesus now proclaims that judgement, says Peter – but with hope of life.

The Catholic doctrine of Purgatory rests upon verses like 1 Peter 4:6, although in its full formulation it says far more: namely that the process of sanctification (becoming holy) continues after death, until we are fit to enter heaven. Peter does not say as much. But we could read Peter's words suggestively in the light of our experience of death in our world – the death of millions in ignorance of Christ, or in opposition to him required by the culture that shapes them, or prematurely before conscious faith is possible. Whether or not we should literally think of Christ preaching the gospel to them after death, 1 Peter 4:6 at least points to the equal treatment of all before God. These dead had been judged in the flesh as everyone is judged (NRSV), but they must be able to give an accounting to God (4:5); and so they hear the gospel, that they might have an opportunity to live in the spirit as God does. We can have the same confidence that the Judge of all the earth will do what is just. (Genesis 18:25).

Easter Day

Acts 10:34–43 *or* Jeremiah 31:1–6; Psalm 118:1–2, 14–24;
Colossians 3:1–4 *or* Acts 10:34–43; John 20:1–18 *or*
Matthew 28:1–10

The readings from both Acts and Jeremiah attempt to describe
God's all-embracing love in the call to be 'The People of God'.
Jeremiah emphasizes the joyful return of all the exiles, forgetting the
division between north and south. What is to be remembered and
celebrated is God's everlasting love and faithfulness in the Exodus
from Egypt and down to the prophet's own day. He promises the
joyful restoration of *all* Israel, including the renewal of pilgrimages
to the Jerusalem Temple.

The Acts passage too places God's salvation on a large canvas: all
the prophets bear testimony to Jesus, and the apostles are witnesses
to his resurrection. The author of Acts is characteristically concerned
with 'eating and drinking': here a foretaste of the final messianic banquet and a reflection on Peter's vision at the house of Cornelius,
which immediately precedes our passage. The continuity from Israel
through Jesus to Peter and to Paul shows a meticulous plan leading
towards the victory of Christianity over the whole earth.

The idea that Christians already participate in the resurrection of
Jesus is unusual in the New Testament. More often baptism is understood as being incorporation into his death, with only Jesus himself
inaugurating the final resurrection in which all will ultimately share.
The letter to the Colossians is therefore exceptional in its confident
affirmation that entry into the new age is already accomplished and
Christians are raised with Christ. The appeal to mind and will is
probably a salutary corollary: new life in Christ is the starting point
for the road to holiness – not its achievement.

The Gospels give us rather different accounts of the story of the
empty tomb: John's continual invitation to a personal relationship
with Jesus flowers in Mary's encounter in the garden. She is commissioned with an apostolic task – which means allowing all that she has
known and understood in the past to be left behind. She must have
her hands free to fulfil the new mission. By contrast, Matthew's
account of the empty tomb is less mysterious, seemingly designed to
overcome doubt with authoritative evidence which will provide the

basis for more confident discipleship. Perhaps Matthew's pastoral instincts suggested that the faith of his community needed protecting from other claims (v. 15 of this chapter suggests rivalry with the Jews of his own day). It has also been mooted that the whole incident of the sealing of the tomb and of the guards is built on two Old Testament passages of which it is seen as the fulfilment, Daniel 6 and Joshua 10. This would certainly be characteristic of Matthew's methods, a way of affirming that all scripture witnesses to Jesus. There is a clarity and an urgency about the instructions both from the angel and from the risen Jesus. And they are heard by the disciples as a body. Members of the Church are the 'true Israel' founded by Jesus in Galilee, the place traditionally of mixed races and 'all nations'.

Background

The story of how Matthew's Gospel came to be written is one that stimulates the imagination. Visualize, if you can, a sunny courtyard somewhere in Syria where the Rabbi Matthew has gathered with a group of refugees from the horrors in Jerusalem (the Temple has been devastated in AD 70). They bring with them the Jewish traditions of the early Church in that city – and discover in their new situation not only fellow believers, who happen to be Gentiles, but also the Gospel of Mark, which has been delivered to them from Rome. This new work is unashamedly radical in its acceptance of non-Jewish believers and in its promise of suffering and persecution for all who follow Jesus. No wonder that the rabbi and his exiled community sit down, with new energy, to scour their scriptures for corroboration of the gospel – and to rewrite Mark's stark story, incorporating their own traditions and insights. We should not be surprised that the Gospel of Matthew sometimes appears to be a patchwork of unresolved dilemmas. Perhaps we can learn from the Easter community in that sunny courtyard about how to live with difference within the body of Christ. Can we, like them, so seek the grace of God that a desert of acrimony may become a place of learning (Deuteronomy 8:2–3)? 'God is preparing for us a springtime of the Church…'(Brother Roger of Taizé).

The Second Sunday of Easter

Acts 2:14a, 22–32; Psalm 16; 1 Peter 1:3–9; John 20:19–31;
OT *alternative*: Exodus 14:10–31; 15:20–21

The seasonal language of creation and new life lies behind all today's readings in one way or another. But the analogy with springtime in the natural world is only appropriate up to a point. The climax of John's Gospel goes further. The disciples are reconstituted as a completely 'new creation', in which Jesus is present as never before. This is the extraordinary dance of God's indwelling – in which all are invited to participate. It's a corporate image: the completion of God's original intention in creation (there is allusion to Genesis), without the limitations of history – yet rooted in the present. God meets us at any time or in any place. Thomas's confession that God is truly revealed in Jesus stands to summarize the gospel as a whole, a reminder that wine jars, miraculous feeding and sight for the blind represent the fruitful and abundant life spoken of by the prophets and celebrated in the Psalms: 'You show me the path of life: in your presence there is fullness of joy.'

Perhaps to underline the continuities which the author maintains between the Old and the New Israel, the tradition is that the Acts of the Apostles takes over from the Old Testament readings in Eastertide. This is a book which begins with the creation of a new Body of Christ at Pentecost (Acts 1:8). The passage set for today is part of Peter's speech and ends with the powerful image of the Church as a 'witnessing community'. The complementary nature of witness and suffering is basic to the New Testament understanding of mission (Acts 5:41), but echoes of martyrdom (the same word in Greek) are lost in translation, and perhaps we only recover the force of the language when we find ourselves similarly up against it.

The Old Testament alternative reading from Exodus describes the deliverance of Israel by God. The God who raised Jesus from the dead is continually saving his people. Their confidence in Moses is dependent on his original call and exaltation by Yahweh, just as the Church claims identification in the new humanity of Jesus. His way in the world is concretely the model for our way of being the new humanity, formed at the beginning of a restoration of cosmic dimensions. The liberation from Pharaoh begins the journey towards the Promised Land, with Moses as the chosen leader.

The second New Testament reading during Eastertide is taken this year from 1 Peter, a letter written to a Christian community under persecution and estranged from the society in which it lives. It is about living hope and present joy for a church established in Jesus's resurrection: called to stand firm and not to retaliate in the face of suffering. The language of rebirth is vivid: the Christian experiences it not simply by being baptized, nor by an obedient lifestyle (though both play their part). It is only by God's grace that anyone can be born anew. The new life is real, but the remainder of the letter will show that there is also a reciprocal demand on Christians to live it out in faithfulness and rejoicing.

History

The Christians addressed by 1 Peter are unlikely to have been members of thriving or large communities. More likely they were little knots of believers dispersed over a wide area. The persecutions do not seem to have been directed by the state. Those of Nero (AD 64) and of Domitian (in the 90s) did not affect this area. More likely they are initially persecuted by members of their own families, their neighbours and friends – afraid of 'difference' – creating a sinister infrastructure, as in the purges of the twentieth century, so that state bullying can depend on networks of fear and betrayal at an intimate level. Later (AD 112) the Roman writer Pliny describes more official intervention in his letter to Trajan (Letters, x.96f) and gives us an insight into his own difficulties in the province of Bithynia. He clearly had doubts about having Christians executed on the say-so of an anonymous informer; they appeared such unlikely people 'of all ages and every rank'.

Third Sunday of Easter

Acts 2:14a, 36–41; Psalm 116:1–4, 12–19; 1 Peter 1:17–23;
Luke 24:13–35; OT *alternative*: Zephaniah 3:14–20

For Luke, the Evangelist, images of pilgrimage are those which predominate in his understanding of the Church's mission. Jesus teaches the disciples 'on the way' to Jerusalem, and in today's Gospel reading the risen Jesus appears to two disciples who are also 'on the way'. The story turns on their blindness and carries echoes of some of the healing miracles in Mark's Gospel, notably Bartimaeus. There are echoes too of the story told by Luke, in Acts, of Paul's blinding on his way to Damascus, and of the conversion of the Ethiopian eunuch on the wilderness road to Gaza. All are followers of 'the Way', and we are called to be their fellow travellers embracing the new life of the broken bread.

The seasonal Acts reading describes the effects of Peter's speech – repentance and baptism – and again the imagery is of a change of direction on the road. Here in Acts, as in Paul's letters, those called to 'repentance' are members of the House of Israel; the language is of return to a known way from which they have strayed. (The Gentiles, by contrast, are later called to turn, for the first time, towards God and away from idols, a different word implying conversion of a more fundamental kind.) This passage combines two dominant themes of Acts: continuity from Israel through Jesus to the apostles, and the portrayal of the Holy Spirit as intervening to secure the spread of the gospel, one which has encouraged Christian disciples from that day to this – but has also on occasion reinforced in us a less attractive kind of imperialism.

This is unlikely to have been the besetting sin of the Christians addressed by 1 Peter. Here the Christian life is described as a time of exile, echoing Israel's desert wandering. The readers are undergoing a fiery trial (4:12) and their alienation is being counteracted by the assurance that, even as Gentiles, they have found a new home and a new family. They are to be active participants, partners in the gracious covenant God has established through Jesus's death and resurrection. These Christians may not conform to the culture that surrounds them but must assume an entirely new way of behaving.

The alternative Old Testament reading is from the prophet

Zephaniah. In this passage the prophet calls on Israel to rejoice in God's presence and the salvation that he promises her, dealing with her oppressors, saving those who are lame and restoring those in the dispersion. This song of 'Joy to Jerusalem' marks the reversal of previous passages. The creation which was to have been swept away is reaffirmed. The message of comfort shares the tone and language of Jeremiah 33 and of Second Isaiah, so although the book presents itself as set in the time of Josiah (640–609 BC), the signs are that is rather later – offering an exilic or post-exilic audience, with a special affinity for the earlier golden age, encouragement in the midst of the rise and fall of empires.

The Psalmist gives thanks for having been brought through life-threatening danger. There is celebration and joy on the other side of his anguish – mixed emotions which compare with those intense highs and lows of the Emmaus travellers described by Luke.

Application.

'The cross has meant despair and disillusionment, not only to Jesus' disciples who had thought in terms of earthly power, but even to those who have shared in some measure his vision of the kingdom. If that is the end of it all, they ask, why waste life? Jesus was either a stranger, they say, in a strange world created by a strange god, or one who was good but lacking the power to make his goodness effective.

'It is the resurrection of Jesus that brings us assurance. It was the risen Lord who inspired his wavering disciples with courage and confidence. They woke up, after the sleep of uncertainty and the spell of despair, to see the living Christ in their midst, to the assurance of the ultimate victory of the cross'.

M. M. Thomas: *The Realization of the Cross*, Christian Literature Society, Madras, 1972

The Fourth Sunday of Easter

Acts 2:42–47; Psalm 23; 1 Peter 2:19–25; John 10:1–10;
OT *alternative*: Genesis 7

To be God's 'flock' in the Bible is about a new way to freedom. When Christians are preoccupied with church structures, we may cease to live the exodus and wilderness journeys which the image recalls. Participation in God's mission then becomes rather blunted. Far from being inspired by the shepherd image to self-sacrifice on behalf of those marginalized and imprisoned, the idea of comforting individual Christians in their pain, important though that be, may lead us towards dependence and lethargy. In the New Testament all shepherding among the flock of God takes the form of suffering servanthood (inspired by Christian reflection on Isaiah 53). Although the Gospel passage shows us much rich growth of interpretation, the chief model is probably Ezekiel 34 where God seeks out his dispersed people and 'feeds them with justice' (v. 16). For the fourth evangelist Jesus is the focal point of God's saving activity. This is a strong image that is only weakened when we become preoccupied with concern for our own security and comfort.

For the author of 1 Peter, God wants Christians involved in the new kind of world he is bringing into being. They were going astray – like sheep – and are no longer to be bystanders, passive and acted upon. They are to be active 'participants', will endure pain while suffering unjustly – just as Christ bore their sins in his body. Like the isolated community addressed by this letter, the Church of our own day must be counter-cultural, though not in an escapist way. Sacrifice, asceticism, modesty, self-discipline and the like, are not popular virtues. We all crave for acceptance by our culture and for a well-defined role within it. But part of our mission will always be to question and challenge prevailing values, inculcating something of the spirit of being 'resident aliens' in the world.

This image of 'homelessness' in the world is complemented by the Acts account of the early days of the Christian movement: a community with its beginnings in Judaism, attendance at the Temple representing its claim to be the 'True Israel'. The results of the feast of Pentecost are the new creation of God's people in unity and mutual care, an idealized picture but one with an engagement with the world.

The story of the great flood, which is the alternative first reading, is about God's judgement upon the wickedness of humankind when the earth is threatened with a return to pre-creation chaos. In the end, of course, 'God remembered Noah' and a new creation is begun. All in all a reminder perhaps that the Lord as Shepherd is primarily the 'saviour' who leads his people into freedom: and that the beginning of salvation is precisely in a good creation in which non-human creatures have their proper place. We cannot afford to exclude the environment from our missionary agenda. As God's judgement took the form of a destructive flood so God's mercy is shown in saving the universe for a new beginning. This is not an historical account – either past or future – but the beckoning opportunity which is given back to us in the present moment.

Interpretation

The book of the prophet Isaiah is more often quoted in the New Testament than any other book in the Hebrew Bible apart from Psalms, and has provided the Church with much of its most familiar language and imagery. Isaiah 53 has given us the tortured Messiah 'like a lamb that is led to the slaughter', and the notion of healing and victory through vicarious suffering. In the early Christian centuries Jesus was portrayed in art as a shepherd, as a child in the arms of Mary, as teacher and healer and as the host at the Eucharist, but he never appears as the one on the cross. The Old Testament prohibition of images may underlie this, and crucifixion was an awesome event at the heart of eucharistic worship. According to the Koran it was not Jesus who was crucified: 'God raised him to himself, God the strong and the wise.' While still holding to this, many Muslims have meditated deeply on Jesus's suffering and readiness to die. There is much power in this mysterious image.

The Fifth Sunday of Easter

Acts 7:55–60; Psalm 31:1–5, 15–16; 1 Peter 2:2–10; John 14:1–14;
OT *alternative*: Genesis 8:1–19

The biblical image of a 'new creation' appears in a variety of forms. There is the new humanity of whom Jesus is the 'pioneer', the ultimate 'New Man' . . . and there is the new body, the Body of Christ, the community called to serve the Kingdom of God. The relationship between 'body' and 'kingdom' is a significant one: there should be signs of the kingdom, making evident in the Church the pull of the future. But the two are not coterminous: when the Church pretends to *be* the kingdom the image completely loses its tension and thus its power to inspire mission.

The pull of the future makes a thematic connection between today's readings. Jesus's departure entails a new relationship between him and the disciples. His earthly mission will be accomplished through them. This passage is the first part of the answer to Peter's question 'Where are you going?', which in turn reflects the problems of the Church serving an apparently absent Lord. If Jesus's departure is his death, then his return is probably to be understood as the resurrection. In which case the reception of the guests into their 'dwelling places' is about the mutual indwelling which is promised to the post-resurrection Church. The centre of interest then moves from Jesus's personal going, the 'Passion', to the 'going' of the disciples along the Christian 'Way' – a way of obedience and adherence to Jesus's example, though not a death which ends the relationship, but rather one which opens it to 'Life'. If Jesus is the way to the Father, then to know Jesus is to know the Father too. There are echoes here of the shepherd parable, allegorized in John 10 in terms of Jesus and the Pharisees. The verse about 'no one coming to the Father' – sometimes interpreted as a warning to those who would choose other ways of faith – is best seen against the background of early Christian anti-Jewish polemic. This is not threat, but reassurance. Jesus's earthly mission will be accomplished through his followers. All who truly come to the Father will recognize, in the message of Jesus, the authentic marks of the God who is revealed.

The stoning of Stephen provides the author of Luke-Acts with a significant turning point in the story of the relationship between the early Church and Judaism. It is told in a way deliberately reminiscent of the death of Jesus in the Gospel – using Psalm 31 (set as today's canticle), underlining the 'martyrdom' (the word means 'witness') to which members of the new community are called – and introducing Saul, who will become the hero of the gentile mission in the second

---

Interpretation

So much damage has been done in the name of John 14:6b, that it is perhaps worth pausing. Few commentators go with the narrow exclusivism which a superficial reading implies, but the debate about the doctrine of the incarnation in relation to a Christian theology of religions goes on. It is no longer possible to read the texts which equate Jesus and God – 'I and the Father are one' and 'Before Abraham was I am' – as verbatim from the mouth of Jesus. The witness of the New Testament writers is diverse and a number of criticisms have been applied to the traditional doctrine; most move away from concentrating on the person of Christ (divine and human) and towards the action of God in Christ. Jesus is accepted as fully a human being. God does not enter his human life from outside, but:

> We see God with the face of Jesus . . . Whom we call God stands behind Jesus, and it is Jesus who gives, as it were, colour, light and *rupa* (form) to God.
> *Vengal Chakkarai, an Indian writer, cited by John Robinson in his* Truth is Two-eyed, *SCM Press, 1979, p.123*

Such an interpretation tends towards recognizing the validity of other great world faiths and supporting open dialogue . The person of Jesus remains central to Christian faith and contributes to that dialogue; but adherents of other faiths also have significant insights to bring. As Tillich put it 'In the depth of every religion there is a point at which the religion itself loses its importance, and that to which it points breaks through its particularity . . .' (cited by Alan Race, Christians and Religious Pluralism, *SCM Press, 1983, p. 148)* half of Acts. The Old Testament option describes the great flood sub-siding – in order that a new creation can emerge.

The reading from 1 Peter is, as we have seen, addressed to a Christian community struggling against harassment, if not overt per-secution. They are reminded of the Church's role as the New Israel. They are to regard their suffering as evidence, not of rejection, but of a call to new responsibility and regeneration by God. Their following of Jesus's way will lead ultimately to life. The image of the people of God as the Temple of God, made up of living stones, carries over-tones of Old Testament final expectation. The build-up of ideas from Exodus, the Prophets and the Psalms serves to convince a Church, which comes from many races and nations, that they can now regard the whole long history of God's people as their own story – a story coming to its fulfilment in them.

The Sixth Sunday of Easter

Acts 17:22–31; Psalm 66:7–18; 1 Peter 3:13–22; John 14:15–21;
OT *alternative*: Genesis 8:20–9:17

According to St John, the incarnation of the Logos reaches its fulfilment in the crucifixion and resurrection of Jesus. The conflict he has with the world is resolved by his incontrovertible victory over the powers of darkness and evil; they thought that they had overcome him by putting him to death, but, in reality, this is his ultimate victory, for he overcame death, and his resurrection means eternal life for all who trust and abide in him. The disciples have certainly had to bear the pain of separation from him for a little while, but his victory is now assured, and it involves and includes them as well.

This is the perspective from which the whole of the New Testament is written: life is changed now that Jesus has been raised from the dead. This is evident from the Acts of the Apostles; Paul's boldness in proclaiming the resurrection of Jesus in the intellectual capital of the ancient world, Athens, marks a high point in his engagement with the culture of his time. He takes seriously the religious scrupulousness which he observes, notes what their own poets say about God, and uses all this as a starting point for his proclamation of Jesus: the god whom they worship in ignorance is the one true God, the Father of Jesus Christ.

Psalm 66 reflects something of Israel's sense of God's presence to all the nations of the world, but quickly returns to those themes associated with the people of God. God may be known by all peoples, but his particular care is the nation which he chose for himself; hence their desire to offer worship which is pure and acceptable. Their knowledge of God assures them that he is ready to hear their prayers and answer them.

The first letter of Peter deals with the question of persecution. Suffering is to be expected by Christian people, the writer says, but they should see to it that they do not bring shame to their faith and their Lord by giving cause to the authorities to punish them for wrongdoing; the proper cause for their suffering the anger of the state must be their confession of faith, and not any kind of criminal behaviour. The point of Jesus's suffering was that he was innocent, and the saving effects of his sacrifice are dependent upon his suffering as the righteous one on behalf of the unrighteous, that he might bring us all to God.

The alternative Old Testament reading, about Noah, is a story of a righteous man whom God preserved from suffering, even when he was punishing the rest of the world for their sin. And after the flood God made a covenant with Noah and promised that he would never again seek to destroy the creation; the rainbow was to be the sign of that covenant.

In these readings the resurrection of Jesus thus provides us with reflection upon the universality of God, the particular love of God for those whom he has chosen to be his own, the necessity of righteous living on the part of those who say they belong to him, and his enduring faithfulness to all people.

Interpretation

1 Peter 3:19 is a puzzling verse. There is no agreement about its meaning. From it, and other New Testament passages (Acts 2:27; Romans 10:7; Ephesians 4:9), we get the phrase 'descended into Hell' in the Apostles' Creed. Visits to the underworld were fairly common in ancient literature – and the 'spirits in prison' have been understood as either the unrepentant dead of Noah's time or the fallen angels of Genesis 6:1–4. These angels were a significant feature of contemporary Jewish thought, so may be in mind; very likely it is all the physically dead who died before Christ could be preached to them. Jesus is also said to have fulfilled 'the sign of Jonah' (Matthew 12:38–41; 16:4; Luke 11:29–32); which presumably relates to Jonah's prayer from the belly of the fish in Jonah 2. Both 1 Peter and Jonah are concerned with the fear of confessing faith before pagans, so this passage in 1 Peter is intended to strengthen the exhortation to bear witness in front of Roman authorities (3:15).

Ascension Day

Acts 1:1–11 *or* Daniel 7:9–14; Psalm 47 *or* Psalm 93;
Ephesians 1:15–23 *or* Acts 1:1–11; Luke 24:44–53

The Ascension, after forty days of resurrection appearances in Luke's story, marks the end of the Easter season. It implies that Christ's humanity is taken into heaven and celebrates his present rule there. Its themes therefore are also concerned with addressing the question of how the twelve disciples are to be upheld in his absence. Generally the readings underline corporate images of the Church.

The first verses of the book of Acts describe the promise of the gift of the Holy Spirit and Jesus's departure into heaven. As Luke's Gospel tells us what Jesus began to do and teach, so Acts tells us what he continued to do and teach by his Spirit. But the Ascension is an essential prerequisite, and Luke tells it twice – once at the end of the Gospel (where it seems to occur on the first Easter Sunday evening), and once, in graphic style, at the beginning of Acts. It is not surprising that his account had such impact on later Christian belief. It seems to have signalled the beginning of a messianic kingdom and, from an early date, his divinity and enthronement with God the Father. Although rare in Jewish tradition, ascent into heaven is recorded in the case of Enoch (Genesis 5:24) and Elijah (2 Kings 2:11) – but in Jesus's case there is also allusion to Psalm 110, celebrating the king seated at the right hand of God – a Psalm much quoted by early Christians.

The earliest preaching soon proclaimed not only Christ's resurrection but also his Ascension and enthronement with God. It meant that he was given dominion over the demonic powers, and so also were members of the Church. Our reading from Ephesians speaks of the 'immeasurable greatness of his power for us who believe', for Christians were united with Christ who is 'far above all rule and authority and power and dominion'. Their death and hidden exaltation was effected through baptism, which Paul in Romans compared to burial and rebirth with Christ (Romans 6:3–4).

The reading from Daniel describes the vision of 'one like a son of Man' (identified with the 'saints/martyrs of the Most High') and the great judgement of the kingdoms of the earth. Although our ways of expressing these things are rather different, the passage affirms that history has meaning and purpose. The saints ('son of Man' is a corporate image) have opportunities to enact in their own lives of righteousness, obedience and martyrdom the reality of God's coming kingdom. The message, like that of Acts, is positive and optimistic. It is this passage which lies behind the Gospel affirmation of Jesus as 'Son of Man', whose obedience leads through suffering to vindication and to a role as judge.

Psalm 47 was regarded as the special Psalm for the New Year Festival. It praises God who has 'gone up' and entered upon his reign over the nations, and the festival seems to relate to the renewal of covenant and so to the realisation of the Kingdom, the goal of history. Similarly, Psalm 93, the alternative canticle, also expresses hope of the kingdom of God, the coming of which is linked to his enthronement: 'Mightier than the thunders of many waters, more glorious than the raging of the sea is the glory of the Lord on high.'

Interpretation

Luke has two Ascension stories: one at the end of the Gospel (his volume one) and the other in Acts (volume two). The two stories are not identical – and this is worth noticing in a writer who is concerned with careful transmission. In contrast to the Passion story, there is little use of Old Testament citations in connection with resurrection in any of the gospels. The scripture texts are those of exaltation and enthronement like Psalm 110:1; Psalm 2:7; Isaiah 55:3; Psalm 118:22. The Gospel traditions of Luke and John agree in linking the missionary activity of the disciples to the bestowal of the Spirit; but Luke's narrative structure requires that Passion, resurrection, Ascension and Pentecost are separate events. Hence the two farewells: one at the end of the Gospel, the other at the beginning of Acts. Possibly Luke knows the same tradition as Matthew of the disciples worshipping the risen Lord (Matthew 28:17); the allusion helps him to his conclusion in the Jerusalem Temple (v. 53) where the disciples spend much of their time in the early chapters of Acts. In the Acts account the Ascension marks the end of the forty days of resurrection appearances and the beginning of a time of prayer, the casting of lots in order to re-establish the New Israel and preparation for the feast of Pentecost.

The Seventh Sunday of Easter

Acts 1:6–14; Psalm 68:1–10, 32–35; 1 Peter 4:12–14; 5:6–11;
John 17:1–11; *OT alternative*: Ezekiel 36:24–28

Jesus's final prayer, before his arrest and trial, summarizes much of the teaching in the rest of John's Gospel – especially as this relates to the mission in which he and his disciples are called to take part. It underlines the theme of obedience by which Jesus reveals the Father's glory. It anticipates his death and asks for God's protection for his followers. The great theme of unity with the Father has been addressed throughout the account of Jesus's ministry. In teaching, in action, and now in his prayer Jesus demonstrates that he and the Father are eternally one.

The story of the Ascension, from Acts, also addresses the question of how the disciples, here corresponding to the renewed tribes of Israel, will be empowered and upheld in anticipation of the coming age. At the beginning of Luke's Gospel Jesus was promised 'the throne of his ancestor David' (Luke 1:32). Here the same author inaugurates the story of the Church by reminding his readers that he would 'restore the kingdom to Israel'. But by now the image of 'kingdom' carries rich allusion to the heart of Jesus's liberating message for debtors and prisoners – the poor and the outcast. The new community is not itself the kingdom – but neither is it something entirely different. Like Jesus's own mission, it is proclaimed in deed and word, and there will be signs of it 'on earth as . . . in heaven'. Much contemporary theology talks about 'the option for the poor' – and that is certainly true of Luke's account of Jesus's mission.

1 Peter seems to be addressed to Christian groups of poor and displaced 'resident aliens' in the Roman provinces of Asia Minor. The problem 1 Peter has addressed is not one of 'spiritual' estrangement – so much as real social conditions exacerbated by Christians' commitment to a new and suspect sect. The primary image for the Church is that of a 'home for the homeless', and these final extracts offer encouragement to these believers through a distinct perspective on the trials they are experiencing. Earlier in the letter they have been invited to rejoice in their suffering because it makes them like Christ. Righteous suffering now brings about unity not only with God and Christ but also with the whole Church. Endurance is to be the occa-

sion for rejoicing and a sign of resistance. Again, as with the other New Testament readings set for today, there is a challenge here for us – to communicate the communal and provisional in contrast to the culture in which we are also called to be, in some sense, 'strangers and pilgrims'.

The Old Testament alternative from Ezekiel reminds Israel that God will restore them and re-form them as his people – with a new heart created by his Spirit within them. 'People of God' reflects the essence of their self-understanding and it is a vision which, in the Exile, became universal in scope. It was an image picked up very early by the followers of Jesus – one that is rich in its allusions to the holiness of God, covenant, repentance, inclusiveness and new life – all the gifts of the Easter season.

Interpretation

Luke's stress on the physicality of Jesus's resurrected body, as the proof of its reality (rather like the 'in bodily form like a dove' at his baptism: 3:22), continues in Acts 1:4 'while he was eating with them' (cf. Peter at Cornelius's house in 10:41). Docetism clings to the belief that Jesus was a divine being who appeared on earth but was not really human (from the Greek dokein, to appear). This removes Jesus from real contact with our humanity and has never been orthodox belief, though it remains a popular way of seeing things, forged by the impact of Greek thinking on Hebrew theology. If Luke's community consisted of both Gentiles and Jews, whose meals together were a source of strife, then the focus on table fellowship as symbolic of the real body of Christ, in flesh and blood, is an added challenge, to us, to embrace difference and try looking at things from another perspective.

Day of Pentecost

Whit Sunday

Acts 2:1–21 *or* Numbers 11:24–30; Psalm 104:24–34, 35b;
1 Corinthians 12:3b–13 *or* Acts 2:1–21; John 20:19–23 *or*
John 7:37–39

There is a build-up of biblical images with which the author of Acts describes the gift of the Holy Spirit at Pentecost. In Jewish tradition it coincides with the gift of the Law – on this day, seven weeks after Passover. In Luke's Gospel John the Baptist had promised a baptism of the Holy Spirit and *fire* (Luke 3:16) – so it is that, in this account, the tongues of flame are a reminder of his call to repentance. The gift of foreign languages suggests the reversal of judgement described in the story of the Tower of Babel in Genesis 11. There is also the suggestion of ecstatic utterance (cf. 1 Corinthians 14:14) in Luke's description of the disciples as 'filled with new wine', although he is generally more interested in the kind of speech which communicates the gospel. And, most vividly of all, the gift of the Spirit to all flesh, and not just to chosen individuals, is a mark of the Messianic age (Joel 2:28–32).

The reading from Numbers describes the Spirit of the Lord being distributed to the seventy elders, enabling them to prophesy. Eldad and Medad represent lay members of God's people – these are not professional prophets. Yet through their prophesying the phenomenon became more widely known, and enabled Moses to give it his public approval. In a way very similar to the New Testament account in Acts, the story suggests a concern to establish a pattern of shared leadership which is sensitive to the voice of the living God.

Psalm 104 is an extended celebration of the goodness of creation – and its order, symmetry and majesty. God has the great sea monster, the forces of chaos, under his constant control. His sustenance is a daily gift to the world.

In Paul's first letter to the Corinthians he is well aware that he is writing to a community in which spiritual phenomena are present. He does not affirm that in themselves these are proof of the activity of the spirit, rather he follows the lead of the Old Testament in claiming that the content of prophecy will be its own vindication. If it is the work of the Spirit of God it will bear witness to the Lordship of Jesus Christ. Christians differ from each other in their gifts; the main point is that all come from the same source and should therefore be the fount of unity rather than of discord. Christians, who are members of Christ, constitute one body.

Whereas the author of Acts envisages tongues of flame, the fourth evangelist sees the Spirit as water 'poured out'. This imagery is never explicitly explained as baptism and it connotes much more than any ritual practice. But it is nevertheless a gift for all. At the end of the Gospel the missionary charge is not, as in Matthew and Luke, a commission to forgive sins so much as the gift of the Spirit. 'He breathed on them' in direct reference to Genesis 2:7, where God makes Adam into a living being, and to Ezekiel 37, where the whole people of Israel are brought back to life by God's Spirit. The risen Christ breathes his life-giving Spirit on the disciples, making them the risen people of God, in whose community the Spirit is alive and active. In this way he promises to make himself present at any time or place. The gift of the Spirit as described in this Gospel brings together the teaching of the New Testament about the presence of God indwelling both the community and individuals.

Application

The continuing struggle to unite across difference – to celebrate difference, to expect pluralism – the message of Pentecost sounds afresh in our own time. Almost certainly the community for which Luke wrote was a mixed one – different in nationality, religious background and economic capacity. Christians in our own day are, of course, called to exercise judgement, in the sense of trying to decide things wisely. But we are never to exercise judgement in the sense of passing sentence on people as people – however differently they see things. That kind of judgement is the prerogative of God. If we want to find faults we should work on ourselves (Matthew 7:1–5). How far have we assumed that we know what people are saying before we even listen to them? And yet we are members of one body! What hope for the world?

Trinity Sunday

Isaiah 40:12–17, 27–31; Psalm 8; 2 Corinthians 13:11–13;
Matthew 28:16–20

Have you ever come to the end of telling a long story and have
someone say at the end of it, 'So what?' We have listened over
the past months to the stories of Advent, Christmas, Epiphany, Lent,
Holy Week, Easter and Pentecost. Now we are entitled to ask,
So what? What does it all mean? In particular, what kind of God is
this?

At Advent and Christmas, we celebrate a God who comes, as
Father of Jesus Christ, with new, creative love into the life and
history of the world. Then in Lent and at the Passion and Easter, we
celebrate the life of Jesus Christ, who is the Way to God, the Truth of
God and the Life of God shared with humankind, even to the point
of suffering and death, so that even all that goes wrong may be forgiven and taken up into the eternal purposes of God. At Pentecost
we celebrate the continuing presence of this God who is Father of
Jesus Christ, alive in every place and circumstance where love and
creativity flourish, and where forgiveness is sought and expressed.

There are three things that need to be remembered today:

1. All these stories belong together, and there is a fundamental unity
in God. Jesus constantly refers to the Father as 'Abba' – 'Dad'. Jesus
had an intimate, adult relationship with the source of all things, and
the kingdom of God is present in his person and life. That is the
implication of all the parables Jesus told and all the stories we have
about Jesus in the Gospels.

The unity between Jesus and God is reflected also in the unity
between all the stories of the Christian Year. We believe in one God,
we say, as inheritors of the tradition of Judaism that saw all things as
depending upon the goodness of one God who creates light out of
darkness and redeems the suffering from evil.

2. The story is about God who moves out to be inclusive. There are
two aspects to this: the first is that the unconditional goodness of
God includes everybody by putting right what goes wrong in life.
The people who were cast out of society for ritual reasons, for

reasons of taboo, for moral reasons – all of them, says Jesus, are included. No one is left out of God's love.

But there is another sense in which the idea of inclusion is important, and it is that early Christians soon came to sense that they were included in the life of God. After the resurrection of Jesus, it was as if God was including them in God's own life; it was as if the very Spirit of God had been given to humankind. So, not only were all human beings included with each other in God's own purposes for human society, all humanity was also included in the life of God. The writer of 2 Peter speaks of our being 'sharers in the divine nature'; and the early theologians of the Church taught that 'humankind is the animal that has received the vocation to become God', and 'God became human, so that humanity might become divine.'

3. So 'Trinity Sunday' is about how human beings are included in the life of God. But just how are human beings included in that life? The answer is, by our behaviour. To put it simply, if we are taken up into God's life, then we are called to behave like God. When we act in unity with God, and are loving and creative, then we show our inclusion in the life of God, and when we refuse to be controlled by the unthinking barriers and taboos of our society and culture, then we are demonstrating our inclusion in the life of God.

Application

There are two things we can do to go on celebrating the Holy Trinity. One is to continue living a life of inclusion, like God, and the other is to recognize the life of God in other people when we see it, and give thanks.

Ordinary Time – Proper 4

Sunday between 29 May and 4 June

Genesis 6:9–22; 7:24; 8:14–19; Psalm 46;
Romans 1:16–17; 3:22b–28; Matthew 7:21–29

The *Lectionary* now directs us to a continuous reading of Matthew's Gospel, from which we have diverted since before Lent. Also to be read continuously are Genesis and Paul's letter to the Romans, from which readings begin today. Passages from the five books of Moses will parallel the story of Jesus, the 'New Moses', while Paul struggles to clarify his conviction that Gentiles can be saved apart from the Jewish Law. All take us, in one way or another, to the distinctiveness of the gospel.

The 'Sermon on the Mount' has repeatedly warned against hypocrisy and pretence – indeed it could be said that this is the emphasis of Matthew's Gospel as a whole, in which all kinds of falsehood are seen as the very opposite of positive discipleship. If for the Jews Moses is the supreme arbiter of the will of God, for the Church it is Jesus. Here, in the conclusion of the Sermon, discipleship means real change, not the adoption of a form of words that might suggest change, but an actual event in the mind and heart. Although this is primarily about God re-establishing a relationship with us, it can also be applied to all our relationships: changes of heart are a result of a new way of seeing things.

Perhaps because he had not met his readers, Paul's letter to the Romans is a more complete and considered writing than any other – and the verses which we read today provide the summary of the whole argument for his mission. His central theme is the universal scope of God's freedom, offered to all who accept it in trust. It is offered not only to Jews but also to Gentiles. This was still an extraordinarily controversial matter amongst Christians – and we miss so much of the radical tone of the Gospel because, for us, Paul's version is the only one we know. That future salvation is anticipated in the present is a key to his thought.

The story of the Flood in Genesis is in some senses the Old Testament precursor of the early chapters of Romans. Here again we hear sounded some of the dominant notes in the faith of Israel:

judgement, salvation and covenant. Picking up from the creation story, this is primarily about the responsibility to which humanity is called and the tragic consequences which stem from our refusal to live up to our calling. The disappearance of the flood water marks the beginning of a new era, which cannot simply be a re-run of the old. The problem and disturbance which human beings bring to the new scenario will continue to be an issue. God's judgement is an ever-present reality. But into this sombre theme there breaks again the note of hope, the echo of Israel's experience of being the object of God's care and love throughout her history.

Text

Beware the Letter to the Romans! It has played a key role in the history of Christianity. Paul, Augustine, Martin Luther and Karl Barth have all applied its teachings to their own times – and our temptation is to fail to see behind their witness to its message for us. There are two short passages set: the first, in 1:16 and 17, a summary of Paul's theology, and the second, in chapter 3, the working out of this in terms of human liberation and the death of Christ. It is worth noticing that although Christian theology has worked out elaborate sacrificial theories, Paul himself does not do so. He alludes to the place of atonement (Romans 3:25), as he alludes to other Old Testament ideas, but does not produce a detailed and consistent theory. Romans 1:17 resembles Psalm 98:2 so closely that the 'righteousness' of God can only be an active and a positive force: it is revealed on the basis of faith alone. Faith, on this view, is not a collection of 'beliefs' but a readiness to let God be God. There are no preconditions for faith: all may believe. The important thing is that God's righteousness is shown to us in the present: a contrast therefore both with the past (and our previous falling short) and also with the future. God chooses to act now, and the present time anticipates the final event. We are reluctant to live up to this calling, frequently unable to act decisively in favour of the freedom and justice to which God summons us. Christianity teaches a challenging view of reality. So often we prefer to buy time and stay safe in our fortress strongholds.

The alternative Old Testament reading is from Deuteronomy, the last of the five 'books of Moses' and clearly related to Matthew's message of loyalty and genuineness of religious practice combined with a just social order. There is an emphasis on the inwardness of true religion and an aim to bring as much of life as possible under God's rule. All this of course accords with Paul's claim in Romans that 'by this faith . . . we uphold the Law'. Psalm 31 also reinforces in a moving way the inner worship of someone moving from fear to confidence in surrender to God. It recalls us to Jesus's obedient surrender on the cross, as described in Luke's Gospel: 'Into your hands I commend my spirit.'

Ordinary Time – Proper 5

Sunday between 5 and 11 June

Genesis 12:1–9 *with* Psalm 33:1–12; *or* Hosea 5:15–6.6 *with* Psalm 50:7–15; Romans 4:13–25; Matthew 9:9–13, 18–26

The God who brings life out of death is celebrated in today's readings. The continuous Gospel moves us on from Jesus's teaching and preaching to the healing aspect of his ministry, highlighted in the restoration of the woman with a flow of blood and of the ruler's daughter. It is difficult for us to feel the full impact which the overturning of the 'blood' taboo represents; the woman certainly risks life and limb by touching Jesus. So both stories are concerned with the power of the gospel to bring life out of death. Matthew places these miracles in a framework that has to do mainly with the theme of following Jesus – the call of Levi, which precedes them, sets the tone. He wants to assure the members of his Church that God-in-Christ, the Life-giver, is present with all those who follow him. Jesus is Emmanuel – 'God with us'. He is in control of all events; nothing happens without his knowledge or consent. 'Lo! I am with you always – to the end of time.'

The Jewish view of Abraham, in the Judaism of Paul's day, has two aspects: he is a model of obedience to God and he is seen as the original recipient of the promise of salvation. He symbolizes privilege and responsibility, and is also a source of hope. Paul is attacking both views, by reinterpreting Abraham so as to give life and hope – not to the Jews, but to the church in Rome. This is not a purely historical discussion – for Abraham believed and was justified, not as an individual, but as the father of believers. The God of Abraham, now made known by a clear demonstration of life-giving power (even clearer than that shown on Mount Moriah in Genesis 22), is the God of Christians. Everything previously said about the faith of Abraham is applied to the faith of believers. The death and resurrection of Jesus show us a God who continually brings life out of death.

Our reading from Genesis marks the beginning of a new section and outlines the basic theme that will run through the rest of the book: a nation embarking on a pilgrimage with God towards the fulfilment of his promise of land, progeny and a name. The journey of faith is energized by memory and vision – so Psalm 33, probably composed for the New Year covenant festival, looks back on past blessings and forward with prayer and confidence to life in the future.

Hosea provides the alternative Old Testament reading, to which Jesus makes direct reference in today's Gospel. The call to repentance, steadfast love and the knowledge of God is closely related to Jesus's mission and supports his assertion that he had come to call sinners, rather than the just – those with no reason to call upon God's mercy. Psalm 50 is a matching proclamation of God's desire for 'true worship'. It is very close to Hosea and the prophetic tradition of the Covenant, the heart of which was not sacrifice but God's revelation of himself, 'that we may live before him'.

Application

There are taboos – different from those of the first century – which twenty-first-century Christians have to confront. Jesus's action may perhaps suggest that our mealy-mouthed excuses about 'timing' and 'getting consensus' do not cut much ice and, in the end, look dishonest. When it comes to women, homosexuals, black people – would Jesus have waited for the Pharisees to write a church report before he acted for their freedom and their full humanity?

Ordinary Time – Proper 6

Sunday between 12 and 18 June

Genesis 18:1–15 *or* Genesis 18:1–15, 21:1–7 *with*
Psalm 116:1–2, 12–19; *or* Exodus 19:2–8a *with* Psalm 100;
Romans 5:1–8; Matthew 9:35–10:23 *or* 9:35–10.8

Matthew's theme of discipleship comes to a significant point with the commissioning of the twelve and the instructions with which they are to set out to the lost sheep of the house of Israel. The image of 'sheep without a shepherd' and of Jesus as 'Good Shepherd' recurs in the Gospels and is best understood against the desert background, a strong liberating God leading his people through the wilderness to freedom in the promised land. When we use it only to comfort the bereaved and the sick, we risk burying ourselves in too passive a religion. By contrast, the mission upon which the disciples

Background

There is a struggle detectable in Matthew's Gospel between the 'orthodox' Jewish Christians, for whom Jesus represents a reform movement, and those who see the Gospel as breaking the bounds of religious and cultural categories more widely. Almost certainly there were Gentiles as well as the Jewish majority. The Christian community is unresolved about an issue that profoundly affects its ability to survive into another century. The question of a 'gentile mission' threatens to tear it apart; the New Testament texts suggest that the followers of Jesus were encouraged to direct their attention to the future Kingdom. For Matthew, disciples pursue their life only in the light of its approach: there is a tension between present and future. Although the Church lives under God's rule, it is not immune to the forces of evil. The focus for its life is to be future-oriented.

embark is in direct imitation of Jesus's own – and promises responsibility, discomfort and self-sacrifice along the way.

Paul too is concerned, in the Romans passage, with the effects of God's gracious action in Jesus. He has discussed, in a complex series of arguments, how justification by faith works and how it involves the union of Jew and Gentile. Now he looks at its consequence: that we 'rejoice in hope of the glory of God', Jew and Gentile together abandoning a limited view of God's salvation. In a meditation on 'hope' Paul describes the many attractive fruits of the Holy Spirit 'who has been given to us'. There are a number of parallels with the Gospel account, not least the sense of the imminence of the end (reinforced by the harvest imagery in Matthew), the urgency of the task and the peace which is its reward. But the primary message to Paul's readers is that they must abandon their restricted view of Jesus – as offering salvation only to them and their particular group!

The birth of a son to Abraham and Sarah begins the fulfilment of God's promises to them. The visitation by the oaks of Mamre is etched in Christian consciousness by the Rublev icon of the Trinity – and the story of Sarah's laughter stands for all time as witness to God's over-ruling in human affairs, only surpassed by the annunciation to Mary in Luke's Gospel. Psalm 116 is one of love and thanksgiving to God. The worshipper's life has been restored – the only response to God's love is a lifetime of commitment.

The alternative Old Testament reading describes the meeting between God and Moses at Sinai – and the people's undertaking to keep the covenant Laws. 'My treasured possession' describes God's special claim upon Israel. Moses's role as the covenant mediator is stressed – the one who represents God to the people and the people before God – making the connection with Matthew's depiction of Jesus as the new Moses leading his disciples into desert places in fulfilment of the new covenant. The call, here as there, is to responsibility and freedom. Psalm 100, sung at the threshold of the Temple, makes an appropriate thanksgiving for God's liberating covenant promises, wherever his people are privileged to embark upon their mission.

Ordinary Time – Proper 7

Sunday between 19 and 25 June

Genesis 21:6–21 *with* Psalm 86:1–10, 16–17; *or* Jeremiah 20:7–13 *with* Psalm 69:7–10, 16–18 *or* Psalm 69:7–18; Romans 6:1b–11; Matthew 10:24–29

The missionary disciples are encouraged to look beyond immediate suffering to the experience of God's fatherly presence. Matthew reminds them that by setting themselves upon ultimate things they will prove that those who kill the body are unable to destroy Life. Paul, in the Romans passage, is also concerned with what lies beyond our immediate experience (in his case the compromised life of sin and limitation) as he begins a long discussion on loyalty to the Jewish Law. Both Matthew and Paul stress the responsibility and struggle to which Christian believers are called. Some must have thought that becoming a Christian was an automatic gateway to the fully realised Kingdom of God. In our less enlightened moments we all look for shortcuts.

Background

Muslims trace their descent from Abraham by way of Ishmael. So what the Bible says about Isaac and Ishmael has a reality, in today's Middle East, that it has not had for centuries. The Israeli poet Shin Shalom draws on the parallel fate of the two brothers, both threatened by death and rescued at the last minute by a divine emissary.

Ishmael, my brother,
How long shall we fight each other?

My brother from times bygone,
My brother – Hagar's son,
My brother, the wandering one.

Matthew had a special interest in the jibe, found in many contemporary writings, that Jesus was a magician and deceiver. His community too is accused of being in league with evil powers, and he warns them that this kind of persecution is to be expected – even welcomed – as part of what it means to be disciples of their Lord. God's presence is to be experienced, as it was for Jesus, as 'fatherly' – going beyond a general sense of 'providence' to a meticulous and loving care.

The discussion of baptism, to which our reading of Romans now brings us, gives an insight into Paul's world view. He understands the 'present age', marked by mortality and constraint, as nearly over. The 'age to come' has been inaugurated by Christ's death, and the resurrection ushers it in. This transition to a world of 'righteousness, peace and joy in the Holy Spirit' (14:17) can, in part, be anticipated by faith through baptism, understood as 'death with Christ'. But the resurrection of the last day will only finally be brought in by the endeavours of Christians to achieve the kind of life to which baptism points. Paul is assuring his readers that to abandon the Jewish Law does not mean casting off all ethical restraint. Grace and obedience are two sides of the same coin.

The continuous Old Testament reading picks up the story of the

One angel was sent to us both,
One angel watched over our growth –
There in the wilderness, death threatening through thirst,
I a sacrifice on the altar, Sarah's first.

Ishmael, my brother, hear my plea:
It was the angel who tied thee to me...

Time is running out, put hatred to sleep.
Shoulder to shoulder, let's water our sheep.

'Ishmael my brother' quoted in *Forms of Prayer for Jewish Worship Vol. III: Prayers for the High Holydays*, Reform Synagogues of Great Britain 1985, p.891

patriarchs with the birth of Isaac, fulfilling God's promise to Abraham, and the banishment of Hagar and Ishmael to the wilderness of Beersheba. This last scene is movingly told – the distraught mother with her dying child, and then the angel bringing hope and a future to the situation. We are to read it as part of the rich tapestry of Israel's pilgrimage of faith. Psalm 86, in the style of an individual lament, moves from supplication to thanksgiving before embarking on another petition in relation to yet another affliction. As for Hagar, there are no guarantees of happy endings in this life.

The alternative reading, from Jeremiah, looks beyond immediate persecution. It begins with a cry of outrage against God which reaches a climax with the denouncing of the speaker by his 'familiar friends' (known to us from the story of Jesus's Passion) and is resolved when God comes to his aid and makes his persecutors stumble. It is unlikely that this lament was ever applied personally to Jeremiah, and it is best read as bemoaning the lot of the faithful community. Psalm 69, also frequently quoted in the New Testament, is another moving testimony to human suffering. It ends – against this background – in grateful praise to God for deliverance, in fulfilment of all creation.

Ordinary Time – Proper 8

Sunday between 26 June and 2 July

Genesis 22:1–14 *with* Psalm 13; *or* Jeremiah 28:5–9 *with*
Psalm 89:1–4, 15–18; Romans 6:12–23; Matthew 10:40–42

There are striking parallels between the first and second readings
set for today. In Romans, Paul struggles to vindicate the place of
obedience in his system of grace and faith. And in Genesis,
Abraham's obedience is precisely an act of faith and opportunity for
a 'gift freely given' by God. This story, like others in the patriarchal
narrative, is best read as part of the rich tapestry of Israel's pilgrimage of faith – and of our own. Isaac represents the whole promise of
the future and, as Israel, is laid on the altar, given back to God, then
given life again by him. We struggle with the strangeness of an alien
world in which God could ask such a thing. But that is not the point:
the pattern of obedience is the one we celebrate Sunday by Sunday in
consecration and in celebration of Jesus's death and resurrection.
Grace must meet with the human response of obedience in order to
lead to salvation. The Canticle, Psalm 13, is a short lament which is
notable for its lack of vitriol and vindictiveness. The prayer ends on a
serene note of confident trust in God's grace – our opportunity to
make the Abraham story our own pledge of obedience.

Called to follow Jesus, the Christians of Matthew's community
know themselves as a band of disciples, in the tradition of the Old
Testament prophets and of Jesus and the twelve. Encounter with the
gospel of the Kingdom precipitates the same crisis for them as it did
for the earthly Jesus. The missionary discourse ends with both warnings and promises. The disciples are to be agents of Jesus, as Jesus
was God's agent. The teaching is then developed to include rewards.
A prophet's reward is vindication (see the Jeremiah reading below),
the promise to the poor in spirit, and those who are persecuted for
righteousness' sake, is entry into the kingdom of heaven (see the
Beatitudes in Matthew 5). Reference to disciples as 'little ones' draws
attention to their political and social powerlessness. Only those who
are meek or humble (5:5), like Jesus (11:29) and like children
(18:3–4), will be able to communicate a gospel to those who are also
materially poor. Offering help to such people could involve the

helpers in persecution too. 'Rejoice . . . for in the same way they persecuted the prophets who were before you' (5:12).

The related Old Testament reading, from Jeremiah 28, is about faithful obedience to the word of the Lord. The prophet of peace can only be vindicated when peace becomes a reality. Hananiah has opposed Jeremiah and prophesied the return from Babylon within two years, and then dies (v. 17) after Jeremiah accuses him of making the people trust in a lie. He is shown to be the false prophet, whereas true prophecy is always obedient to God's word. This is celebrated in

---

Reflection

'We are all used to slow motion. At some important event in the film, time is stretched out for us to an unbearable extent by running everything at a slower speed, delaying the climactic moment. The identical technique can be seen at work in the story of the 'Binding of Isaac' in Genesis chapter 22. The three days' journey that Abraham has to undertake is glossed over with a few words, but the act of preparing to kill his son is spelled out in incredible detail, each verb being stretched out to hold the suspense even longer.

> *They came to the place of which God had told him and*
> *   there Abraham built an altar*
> *And he laid out the wood*
> *And he bound his son*
> *And he placed him upon the altar above the wood*
> *And Abraham stretched out his hand*
> *And he took the knife to slay his son.*
> *Then called to him a messenger of the Eternal from*
> *   heaven, saying, "Abraham, Abraham!"*
> *He said, "Here I am!"*

'We are with Abraham in every detail and at every moment up to the very last second when the voice comes to prevent him. The writing itself suspends time.'
(Jonathan Magonet, A Rabbi's Bible, SCMPress, 1991, p. 77)

the Canticle, from Psalm 89, which speaks of God's faithfulness to the covenant, of the righteousness he imputes to his people and the protection with which he shields them.

Ordinary Time – Proper 9

Sunday between 3 and 9 July

Genesis 24:34–38, 42–49, 58–67 *with either* Psalm 45:10–17
or Song of Solomon 2:8–13; *or* Zechariah 9:9–12 *with*
Psalm 145:8–14; Romans 7:15–25a; Matthew 11:16–19, 25–30

What is lacking in the Old Testament reading is the fact that Abraham's servant's speech is a repeat of the narrative in the first half of Genesis 24. The scriptures present us with the repetition which enables the story to become fixed in the readers' and hearers' minds, so that, as the servant tells the story, we can almost mouth the words for him, for they are so familiar. Nor is this repetition without its point. Here is one of the foundation stories of Israel's history; God is in the process of fulfilling his promise to make Abraham's descendants 'as numerous as the sands on the sea-shore'.

We see the servant's sense of helplessness at his task, his turning to prayer, the serendipitous way in which Rebekah appears just as he finishes his prayer. We may be surprised at her apparent readiness to return with the servant and so few guarantees as to his good intentions; but such complexities are not for the narrative of Israel's salvation. She willingly goes and becomes Isaac's wife.

The Psalm picks up the theme of the bride willingly leaving her own home in order to join her husband's household; and the alternative Canticle, from the Song of Songs, is a delightful love song, gentle in its light eroticism, which celebrates the love of a woman for her husband.

The reading from Zechariah paints a picture of royal humility. The king does not ride on a horse, which would be a sign of triumph, but on a donkey. This could well be a reference to those parts of the temple worship which included the ritual humiliation of the king prior to his subsequent raising to honour and glory. Such a reading makes good sense of the final promise, 'today I declare that I will restore you double.'

In his exposition of his understanding of the gospel in the letter to the Romans Paul is explaining the nature of human experience. What he writes could almost stand as the heading to anyone who ever wrote their 'Confessions', from St Augustine onwards. Here the apostle speaks of the divided nature of his desires: he wants both to do right and to gratify his baser desires by sinning. There are those who say that this passage refers to Paul's, and therefore human, experience before conversion. The context, however, would suggest that the experience related is intended to be both universal and a permanent feature of human living; in the all-too-human struggle to do what is right, God's victory is known through Jesus Christ, preventing, restoring and redeeming. Whether he does one or the other, the praise is due to him.

That is why the yoke of Christ, ultimately, is easy and his burden light. In all the confusions of life it is impossible to please everyone. There will always be those folk who will refuse to join in our joy, whether we play weddings or funerals. When it seems that those around us are intent upon finding something to whinge about, the children of God and followers of Jesus can give thanks for the insight they receive into the nature of the human soul. Such turning in thankful prayer results in the recognition of one who always welcomes us with the embrace of compassion and consolation. What God demands of us – the yoke of the Law was enjoined upon the people of Israel – is our joy and pleasure, for it speaks of a relationship begun in God's grace, continued in God's favour and to be concluded in God's eternal delight.

Application

Donald Nicholl (*Holiness*, DLT 1987, p. 26) tells of a Muslim woman mystic, Rabi'a, who lived a thousand years ago in Baghdad. She was asked by her followers how to achieve the virtue of patience, and simply replied, 'Stop complaining.' It took her colleagues some time to realize that, much of the time, they were unhappy because they complained, not the other way round.

Ordinary Time – Proper 10

Sunday between 10 and 16 July

Genesis 34 *with* Psalm 119:105–12; *or* Isaiah 55:10–13 *with*
Psalm 65 [1–8] 9–13; Romans 8:1–11; Matthew 13:1–9, 18–23

The story of Jacob's supplanting of Esau is put right back at their birth. The struggle in which they engaged as they emerged from the womb skilfully sets the scene for their relationship in later life. Much is made of the meaning of their names: Esau, a name with no clear etymology, is linked with the word for 'dark-skinned', or 'red-haired', and also the tribal name 'Edom'; and the name Jacob, which probably means something like 'may God protect', is made a pun on the word 'heel'.

Alongside Jacob's conniving there is Esau's disdain for his birthright. Psalm 119 seems to mock both of them. The Psalmist sings the praises of God's Law and re-affirms his own attachment to studying and obeying it.

Isaiah 55 begins the third section of the book of Isaiah with an assurance of the reliability of God's promise to establish peace, prosperity and fruitfulness. Psalm 65 is a clear statement of God's power in creation and control of the destiny of nations.

Paul's development of his argument of Romans has reached the point at which he speaks of the work of God's Spirit. Having explained his thanks that God in Christ provides deliverance from – or perhaps, within – the tensions of the moral life, he asserts that the cross of Christ means the absence of condemnation. It is by the Spirit that Jesus was raised from the dead, and the 'Spirit' principle has set us free from the 'Law' principle. Believers in Jesus are not bound by what controls the lives of those who live only ' in the flesh' (and that includes both Jew and Gentile), for the Spirit of God has brought about a new state of affairs. In raising Jesus to life by the Spirit, and, by implication, the whole of humanity with him (since he is the second Adam), God has established a new, Spirit-centred form of human existence. Believers in Jesus, that is, those who have perceived and appropriated this truth for themselves, are therefore free from the flesh and all that belongs to it, including the Law, and sin, and death.

The parable of the sower may be read as another angle on the work of the Spirit. The Word of God is active in creation and redemption in the Old Testament. For Paul it brings about saving faith in Jesus. In the context of the conflict which characterised the life of Jesus it is a secret and hidden thing; whether or not it takes root, sprouts up, develops and comes to maturity depends upon the reception it receives. While the gospel is for all, it also demands assent from those who hear it.

Application

Assent to God's Word is also demanded from those who profess to have responded to it already. Having thus responded, we are required and invited to allow our continuing response to permit growth until the harvest.

Ordinary Time – Proper 11

Sunday between 17 and 23 July

Genesis 28:10–19a *with either* Psalm 139:1–12, 23–24 *or*
Wisdom of Solomon 12:13, 16–19; *or* Isaiah 44:6–8 *with*
Psalm 86:11–17; Romans 8:12–25; Matthew 13:24–30, 36–43

The story of Jacob is ample evidence for the notion that men and women do not earn God's favour, for it is given freely in spite of, rather than because of, what we do. Jacob, enjoying his father's favour after cheating his brother of his birthright and blessing, stops for a night's rest on his way to find a wife from his father's own tribe. While he is on the way, God appears to him. And not only that: God reveals himself as the God of his ancestors, Abraham and Isaac. He promises to be with him, to make his descendants as numerous as the dust of the earth and to give him and his descendants the land promised to Abraham. Jacob awakens from the dream in which this revelation was made to him and recognizes that he has met with God. The image is of heaven opened and its secrets revealed; this is the plan of God for him.

Psalm 139 is an appropriate reflection upon God whose love for his people goes hand in hand, both with intimate knowledge of them and with universal presence and companionship. The readings from both the Wisdom of Solomon and Isaiah speak of the uniqueness of God. Along with his unquestioned power and authority go his consistent compassion and care for his people; so his love is strong and his insight is merciful. According to Third Isaiah he is unique among the gods in that he tells the end from the beginning; his prophecies come true, and his promises are certain of fulfilment.

Well may the Psalmist pray, 'Teach me your way, O Lord, and I will walk in your truth; knit my heart to you, that I may fear your name.' Knowledge of and relationship with this God is a source of confidence and a guarantee of security. The Psalmist's opponents may well 'rise up' and commit violence, but his confidence is in God, whose help is assured, on the basis of his previous faithfulness.

St Paul does not say to the Romans, in so many words, 'we are debtors to the Spirit,' but that is the implication of his argument; because it is the Spirit of God who raised Jesus from the dead, and because, as he has just said, the Spirit of God lives in them. Therefore they are obliged to live and to be led by the Spirit. What is more, this Spirit, who lives within them, is the one who prays through them. It is the Spirit within who acknowledges the Father of Jesus Christ as the Father of the believer. This is a most intimate statement of the union which Christians enjoy with God – as intimate as that of Jesus himself with his Father. Perhaps nowhere else does Paul come so close to asserting that the Christian believer takes on the divine nature. The implications follow logically, but are profound in their import: first, the suffering of the believers is part of the suffering of the whole of creation till it is perfected in Christ; second, their prayers are the groaning of the very Spirit of God, who longs for the fulfilment of all things; third, the hope which is set before us is the ground, not of impetuousness, but of patience.

Using very different imagery, the parable of Matthew 13 suggests that the fruits of the Kingdom of God cannot but live alongside the fruits of opposition to its claims. It is for God to judge what is of lasting value. When that judgement is made, those who are regarded as righteous will 'shine like the sun'.

Application

The convictions that suffering will issue in the perfection of the whole of creation, that prayer is the groaning of the Spirit of God, and that hope makes not for impetuousness, but patience, are difficult to maintain in a world which we today construe very differently. However, the insight is clear enough: the realm of the divine is the true home of the believer. Certainly, the divine has taken up residence in the human, but God's values, of righteousness, of patience, of alertness to the life of the Spirit, are what are called for.

Ordinary Time – Proper 12

Sunday between 24 and 30 July

Genesis 29:15–28 *with either* Psalm 105:1–11, 45b *or* Psalm 128; *or* 1 Kings 3:5–12 *with* Psalm 119:129–36; Romans 8:26–39; Matthew 13:31–33, 44–52

The reading from Genesis finds Jacob still on his quest for a wife – or two. He is about to discover that in his uncle Laban he has also found a match for his own cunning. The writer skilfully juxtaposes the two sisters; he does not say that Leah was ugly, for he mentions her lovely eyes, but he clearly prefers Rachel – as did Jacob – 'for she was graceful and beautiful'.

There was a convention among Laban's people that older sisters should marry before younger ones. So Jacob completes the week required to consummate his marriage with Leah, and then Rachel is given to him as well. The theme of trickery around the whole life of Jacob will continue into his later life and his dealings with his sons. Through it all, however, the promises of God will be worked out, and his descendants will become as numerous as the stars in heaven, as the sand on the sea-shore and as the dust particles on the earth. God solemnly keeps his promises; but he does not lack a sense of humour.

That is the context for the Psalmist's recollection of God's faithfulness to Abraham, Isaac and Jacob. Having once promised that they and their descendants would possess the land of Canaan, he keeps his word. In the context of the alternative Psalm 128, the statement, 'Your wife shall be like a fruitful vine within your house, your children like olive shoots round about your table', might also sound a little ironic; Jacob found himself with two wives within a week. But the number of his children was certainly a reminder of the goodness of God.

The reading from 1 Kings has as its background the faithfulness of God to the house of David, for it speaks of the continuation of the Davidic line through his son, Solomon. Here is the well-known story of Solomon's request for 'an understanding mind', so that he might discern between good and evil as he governs God's people. He is certainly given wisdom and understanding, so much so that he becomes a byword for his wisdom; but God adds to this gift those things, such as riches and honour and victory, which he did not ask. The chosen section of Psalm 119 reflects, not upon Solomon and his wisdom, but upon the Law, which came later to be seen as the fount of all wisdom.

St Paul's argument in Romans moves on to the great themes of prayer and assurance. He teaches that, when believers pray, it is the Spirit of God within them who does the praying. Indeed, the implication is that the Spirit of God is at work praying within us even as we are not consciously at prayer. This is the basis of the Christian's assurance; the divine Spirit is at work in human lives, assuring us of our acceptance in the sight of God, of our freedom from condemnation for all and any sins, and of the final victory within and among us of the resurrecting and transforming power of God. Nothing will tear us from his powerful embrace.

The meaning of the collection of parables in Matthew 13 is not at all clear. It could be that they all highlight a series of contrasts: between the size of the mustard seed and that of the great tree into which it grows; then of the small amount of yeast and of the large loaf of bread which it produces; then of the value of the many pearls which the merchant sells in comparison with the one valuable pearl which is worth more than them all. The final image of the net which catches a large haul of fish then changes the focus onto the outcome at the last judgement of the choices which people have made. The point of the last statement is a reference to Jesus's own teaching style, which consists of a series of contrasts. Are we to reckon that what Jesus teaches is what is new, and the background against which he does so comprises what is old? Or does he use both the new and the old to underline his message of the newness of the Kingdom of heaven?

Another alternative is that there is progression through all these parables, and that the two earlier ones are still concerned with growth, but that the second two are about the proper response to his teaching; those with insight into its value will give up all their belongings to possess what is the pearl of great value; the parable of the dragnet then comments on the wise choice that they have made. Thus Jesus is able to comment on the variety of his teaching – or, perhaps, the Evangelist is able to put into the mouth of Jesus a comment about how he taught. Whatever it is, what is new and what is old mixes to form the stories that will engage the listeners and so make them respond to the demands of the kingdom.

There is a third possibility. That is that the teaching set out here is designed by the Evangelist to engage the reader at different levels, that they are not to be read allegorically at all, but should be allowed to have their effect as parables in whatever way they will. The final statement probably refers, not just to this collection of sayings, but to what has preceded it in the whole of the Gospel story so far. What is old in the teaching of Jesus is his passion for the kingdom of heaven; what is new is the particular emphasis he places on it and the allusive manner of his teaching.

Application

Whatever is the correct reading of these parables, the reader is invited to engage with the good news of God's coming kingdom and to be prepared to follow Jesus into it, whatever it may hold in store. The earlier lessons today will remind us that God may be trusted to see that we are loved, cared for and supported, so that judgement may come, but God's kingdom, initiated in Jesus, will include our salvation.

Ordinary Time – Proper 13

Sunday between 31 July and 6 August

Genesis 32:22–31 *with* Psalm 17:1–7, 16; *or* Isaiah 55:1–5 *with*
Psalm 145:8–9, 15–22; Romans 9:1–5; Matthew 14:13–21

The story of Jacob wrestling with the unknown man is another of
those stories which have become classics. Here is a man who hitherto has got his way by cheating and deception. Now his brother,
whom he has defrauded of his birthright, has at last caught up with
him, and he expects conflict. He moves his wives, children, servants
and goods to the other side of the river and waits for daybreak and
the inevitable confrontation. However, we are suddenly told that 'a
man wrestled with him until daybreak.' We do not learn who the man
was, nor where he came from, nor how the fight started. What we do
learn is of Jacob's tenacity, which is such that the unknown wrestler
can only do Jacob a permanent injury in order to assert his superior-
ity. Still Jacob refuses to loose his hold, for he perceives that he needs
this stronger man's blessing before he proceeds to meet his brother.

The blessing comes in the form of the question, 'What is your
name?', and Jacob gives it. But something has happened to him in
this all-night wrestling match; he has changed from the cheat and
supplanter into one who struggles with God, so his name is changed
to Israel, 'Prince-with-God'. Jacob asks for his assailant's name, and
in being told to mind his own business he is made aware that it is
God who has taken him on. So this night has been the night in which
he grew up, in which he took on God and survived, in which he
earned a new name – and as a result of which he now walks with a
limp. Yet was there ever a more promising sunrise?

If Psalm 17 is read as a commentary on this narrative, we may
note that the 'innocence' of which the poet speaks, if it is to apply to
Jacob, is an innocence which is imputed rather than demonstrated.
The favour of God involves a clean slate, and the person who has
met and struggled with God may rightly call upon God and expect
an answer, and see more of his 'marvellous loving-kindness'. Such
goodness on the part of the God who grants us to see his likeness,
and whose presence 'satisfies us early' has as its purpose the con-
forming of our will to his own loving purposes.

The prophet whom commentators have come to know as Second Isaiah ends his prophecy to the nation of Israel with an invitation to return to God; the prophecy is about their return to the land, but their return is not complete until they come back to God. The prophet is aware of the nation's tiredness and frustration, and he offers a new start. The people are thirsty and poor, and their economy is failing, but the solution to their ills is to be found not in financial management but in addressing the deeper, spiritual issues which face the people and their leaders. The prophet speaks of the covenant with David and suggests that it is within this context and this memory that their salvation lies.

In the context of this Old Testament lesson the Psalmist is heard to sing of God's faithfulness and compassion. When the people are hungry he feeds them, and when they call upon him he will answer.

In the letter to the Romans St Paul continues his explanation of the gospel he has preached, and now addresses the issue of the place of the nation of Israel in God's purposes. Now that God is known in Jesus Christ, what is the place of Paul's own people, the Jews? If only they could be saved, says Paul, he would willingly forgo salvation himself. The question will be worked through over the next three chapters of the letter, but we do well to bear in mind that this is the spirit in which Paul writes.

Today's Gospel tells the familiar story of the feeding of the five thousand. We might note: (a) that the Evangelist sets it in the context of the death of John the Baptist; (b) that it begins in Jesus's com-

---

Theology

All these readings today say something of God's people, the Jewish nation, and the constant nature of his goodness in his dealings with them. From the time of the patriarchs and his initial call of them, through the trauma of exile and return, in Paul's agonizing over the nature of the gospel and in Jesus's compassion for them, we see the character of God towards one nation whom he delights to call his own. In Jesus that call comes to all nations and all people, and his love and grace are as constant and reliable as ever.

passion for the people's hunger, after he has already shown his compassion for their sicknesses; (c) that the miracle is performed, not with miraculous food, but with a small amount of what is already available; (d) that his actions both reflect Jewish practice in giving thanks for food and also, thereby, echo his actions at the Last Supper; (e) that the leftovers, in twelve baskets, presumably reflect the numerical symbolism of the twelve tribes of Israel. In St Mark's Gospel this story is clearly designed to indicate Jesus's feeding of Israel, and there is a second, in gentile territory, which speaks of the wider appeal of the good news. Matthew simply omits the second, speaking of Jesus, therefore, as the one who, in himself, sums up Israel's life and provides nourishment for her. The very large number may perhaps be taken to symbolize the whole nation, while the reference to John the Baptist reminds us of his preaching to the people and his demand that they repent; he looked forward to Jesus (Matthew 3:11ff), and here Jesus takes on his mantle.

Ordinary Time – Proper 14

Sunday between 7 and 13 August

Genesis 37:1–4, 12–28 *with* Psalm 105:1–6, 16–22, 45b; *or*
1 Kings 19:9–18 *with* Psalm 85:8–13; Romans 10:5–15;
Matthew 14:22–33

The story of Joseph gives the lie to the myth of the sanctity of
family life. Families have their tensions, and their emotions can
run to the murderous. Jacob's domestic arrangements were not made
simpler (a) by his having two wives and (b) by his also fathering
children on his wives' maids. Joseph and Benjamin were the sons of
Rachel, their father's favourite wife. Bilhah, who was Rachel's maid,
was the mother of Dan and Naphtali. Leah's maid was Zilpah, and
she was the mother of Gad and Asher.

As the first son of Jacob's favourite wife, Joseph was himself a
favourite, and his behaviour did nothing to endear him to his
brothers: his father bought him a special coat, and Joseph's insuffer-
able conduct included telling his brothers that he had had a dream in
which the whole of the rest of the family bowed in reverence before
him. The plot to kill him was easily hatched, and only the quick
thinking of Reuben (the first son of Leah, Jacob's first wife, so the
most senior of the brothers) saved Joseph from death. Judah was the
third son of Leah, and he contrives to ensure that Joseph is not killed
but sold into slavery; the brothers will have cause to be thankful in
years to come that they spared his life.

Psalm 105 recounts Joseph's story as part of the recollection of
God's mercies and his faithfulness to his people; frequent recitation
of narrative fixes the story in the mind and causes the worshippers to
continue in thanksgiving and constancy in keeping their side of the
covenant with God.

Elijah had good cause to feel depressed. His triumph over the
prophets of Baal seemed short-lived; and, as frequently happens, his
experience of mountain-top elation was followed by one of utter
despair. Sensing he is alone in his zeal for God, he wishes he were as
dead as the false priests whom he had killed. God knows enough psy-
chology to be aware that what Elijah needs is a dose of reality: the
reality of his presence alongside a sense of what is really going on. So

he stages a spectacle of seismic and elemental power, only to indicate that these forces, though they operate at the divine behest, are not the fullness of God's self-disclosure. The translation, 'a sound of sheer silence', correctly captures the paradoxical mystery of God's address to him; God is to be identified in this silent voice of a spoken stillness. All Elijah can do is repeat his complaint, but this elusive God calls his prophet to further action; only then will Elijah know that God is still God.

In this way, as the Psalmist celebrates, God speaks peace to his faithful people; his salvation is near to those who are prepared to wait for the clamours to cease and for the silence to speak; mercy and truth yield to their mutual embrace as God silently communicates his continuing love.

St Paul is also approaching mysteries when he says that the gospel is more than obeying the Law, even though that Law was a gift of God's grace. Now that Christ has appeared and been raised from the dead a new life principle has been established. His exaltation to heaven does not require anyone to attempt to bring him down, any more than his death requires anyone to descend into the grave to find him. His life is a spiritual reality known at first hand, accessible to the touch of any human spirit which dares to confess faith in Jesus. To confess him is to call upon him, and to call upon him is to know that we have already received and heard his call to us.

What glorious good news this is to a tired and struggling humanity: rest and ask for grace, and grace will be given. Paul echoes Isaiah 52 with his exclamation, 'How beautiful are the feet of those who bring good news!' The messengers of such a gospel are so transformed by what they carry that they appear to be as desirable as the message they bear.

St Matthew's story of the stilling of the storm alters the account in

Application

How easy do we find it, both to rest in the knowledge of God, and to know when not to rest, but to strike out in faith in some new enterprise?

Mark upon which it is dependent. The context is of the miraculous feeding of the five thousand. The disciples must have been accustomed to the sudden storms for which the Sea of Galilee was and is notorious. We are told that the purpose of the incident is to test their faith: it is Jesus who makes them go across the lake, and he criticizes their lack of faith when they become afraid. Mark has the disciples 'utterly astounded, for they did not understand about the loaves, but their hearts were hardened', whereas Matthew has a more definite confession of faith, 'Truly you are the Son of God.' For the Evangelist, Jesus acts like God in his capacity to control even the chaotic forces of primal nature.

Ordinary Time – Proper 15

Sunday between 14 and 20 August

Genesis 45:1–15 *with* Psalm 133; *or* Isaiah 56:1, 6–8 *with* Psalm 67;
Romans 11:1–2a, 29–32; Matthew 15:(10–20) 21–28

Years have passed in the story of Joseph since he was sold into
slavery, and he is now able to save his brothers from the effects
of the famine which has ravaged the land. Twice they have come to
Egypt for corn, and he has played with their emotions every bit as
much as they, years before, made light of his youthful suffering. Now
he can bear the pretence no longer; he has made them return to Egypt
after their second visit by having a valuable cup 'planted' in
Benjamin's sack of food. Terrified, they return, only to be told the
almost incredible truth that he is their brother, and that the divine
purpose behind their ancient trickery and malice was that the family
might be spared the famine by God's providence – and, we may say,
greater deliverance might be demonstrated by the escape from the
slavery in Egypt that will follow.

Those who know earlier translations of Psalm 133 will perhaps be
amused that the perfectly valid inclusive language translation of the
New Revised Standard Version omits any reference to 'brothers' living together in unity; 'family', while not incorrect, misses the point of
the particular association here. 'Fine oil' would be sweetly perfumed,
and the anointed priest represents the whole people, acceptable and
ready to stand before God in worship.

Isaiah offers a vision of all nations coming to Jerusalem to worship
God, as long as the people, now returned to their holy city from exile
in Babylon, act justly and do what is right. Upon the righteous
behaviour of the people of God depends the salvation of the world.
The words of the *Deus Misereatur*, in Psalm 67, pick up the theme of
the nations' knowing God's saving health. Here there are no conditions, however, only unadulterated joy in the praise of God.

St Paul injects a personal note into his arguments that Israel, God's
chosen people, is by no means cut out of God's purposes by the
coming of Christ, even if the chosen people reject the chosen Son.
God does not go back on his promises or his call.

The passage omitted from the shorter reading of the Gospel provides the background to the story of the Canaanite woman. Jesus is asserting that the food laws, which are concerned with 'what goes into the mouth', are less important than moral behaviour, that is, what comes out of the mouth and heart, in speech and in action. The Pharisees in the story symbolize adherence to the ritual taboos which Jesus regards as unimportant. The Canaanite woman would have been regarded as unclean, for the Canaanites were one of the nations which the Israelites were commanded to drive from the land at the time of the conquest under Joshua – and she was also a woman, and therefore naturally inferior! Jesus's initial response to her is brusque and unkind, and his use of the imagery of food is telling. The woman, however, reacts with wit and humour, and Jesus commends her spirit as evidence of faith. He promptly effects the exorcism of the demon which troubles her daughter. The immediacy, spontaneity and surprise of the miracle are characteristic of the presence of Jesus, who embodies the kingdom of God.

Application

What are the groups of people in our society that are rejected and regarded as less than human? If we are to live the gospel as Jesus calls us to do, we must become aware that the taboos and exclusions which all societies effect – sometimes with the active support of the Church – are against the spirit of the good news of Jesus Christ.

Ordinary Time – Proper 16

Sunday between 21 and 27 August

Exodus 1:8–2:10 *with* Psalm 124; *or* Isaiah 51:1–6 *with* Psalm 138;
Romans 12:1–8; Matthew 16:13–20

The great saga of Israel's history continues with the story of the birth and background of Moses. Fear of the rapidly growing community which has descended from Joseph's brothers leads Pharaoh to his racist policies. Fortunately the Hebrew midwives are sufficiently cunning to outwit him, and even Pharaoh's own daughter cannot resist the charm of the little baby she discovers among the reeds on the riverbank. Equally cunning is the baby's sister, who contrives that her brother is nursed by his own mother, and then introduced to the Egyptian court when he is old enough. Names are important in the Bible, and the name 'Moses' is probably of Egyptian origin, but it is taken here to be cognate with the Hebrew 'to draw out' (i.e. from the water).

The Psalmist gives thanks to God for his timely help; the people have escaped because God has been on their side. Read or sung on this day, the Psalm arouses us to give thanks for all the serendipitous and timely events that pattern our lives. The passage from Second Isaiah is a characteristic celebration of divine salvation as the nation looks towards the promise of return from exile, and Psalm 138 celebrates the constancy of God's care for his people.

St Paul's 'Therefore . . .' in Romans 12:1 is one of the great 'consequences' of Christian literature. The previous eleven chapters have spelled out the magnificence of the gospel as Paul understands it. In Christ all people, though potentially guilty before God, if not on the basis of Law, then certainly at the bar of conscience, stand not condemned but freely and utterly forgiven.

The work of Christ, effected through the cross, demands an appropriate offering in return. So Paul coins this stunning image of the 'living sacrifice'. Usually, sacrifices are dead; not because death is pleasing to God, but because life was thought by the Jews to reside in the blood, and life must be offered. When blood is shed, the sacrifice dies; but the blood of Christ has already been shed, so the offering of Christian people is the offering of a sacrifice which is paradoxically and gloriously alive. The company of believers is called to live the life of offering and spiritual sacrifice.

The paradox of a 'living sacrifice' suggests the transformation from death to life, just as it mirrors the sacrifice of Jesus in his life to the point of death. So believers are called to live 'sacrificially', allowing their assumptions, their hopes, their expectations and their behaviour to be as transformed into Christ-likeness as his body was transformed, first to death, then to risen life. So they die to themselves in order to live for each other.

This same fundamental precept underlies the significance of the life of Jesus. The passage in Matthew 16 is the preamble to Jesus's statement about the centrality of suffering in discipleship. The Messiah, or Christ, the Son of God, may have represented to Peter the optimistic fulfilment of all his hopes, but to Jesus himself as narrated, it is a title which involves salvation through a cross, and resurrection only after death. The 'power of the keys' is no passport to painless power; it is the way into untold suffering, and only then to glorious life again.

Application

The acknowledgement in Christian theology of the inevitability of suffering and of the possibility of its transformation can lead both to a cruelty which has, at times, been all too willing to inflict suffering, and to an insensitivity which too early suggests that those who suffer should trust in God and so act as though the pain were not as bad as it is. Such an approach is far removed from Christian compassion. Human suffering is real, and we do God no favours by encouraging folk to think otherwise; most of us learn only gradually of the love of God that comes to us through what we suffer. The lesson cannot be forced.

Ordinary Time – Proper 17

Sunday between 28 August and 3 September

Exodus 3:1–15 *with* Psalm 105:1–6, 23–26, 45b; *or*
Jeremiah 15:15–21 *with* Psalm 26:1–8; Romans 12:9–21;
Matthew 16:21–28

The story of the call of Moses is a major milestone in the account of Israel's relationship with God. The story which gives the reason for Moses's being in Midian is given in Exodus 2. He has fled there after being recognized as the man who killed an Egyptian. He had become aware of his Hebrew birth and had stood up for a fellow Hebrew who was being abused. So he has settled in Midian and married. The tale of the experience he has with God is to prove foundational for Hebrew thought and Christian theology for centuries to come.

There are two basic paradoxes here. The first paradox is the bush which is burning but not consumed. The second is of God's name. The word translated 'Lord' is impossible both to pronounce and to translate. Both spellings, 'Jehovah' and 'Yahweh', are inadequate renderings of what cannot be said; and there is much speculation as to the origin of the name – including the idea that it represents a Midianite God called Yah.

However, in the text the name is made to relate to the Hebrew for 'to be', and by changing just two of the four root letters, the form 'I am' is produced. The point would appear to be that the name of God is profoundly mysterious. The name expresses the character, so we are dealing here with what is complete mystery, because we are dealing with God. Nevertheless there is a sense in which God may be known, and that is in his actions. When he says 'I am that [which] I am,' he is not cloaking himself in some further abstruseness; nor is he beginning a tradition of abstract reflection on the nature of 'being'. He is saying that he will be shown to be living in the world in which all other things and beings live, by taking action. In particular, his action will be the deliverance of the people from slavery.

It is this that is celebrated in Psalm 105. God is not an abstract being who is to be thought of 'beyond' this world; he is present in the world and to it and within it, for he brings about change and is at work in the lives of men and women to effect deliverance and salvation. What these terms mean is spelled out in the stories of nations and people.

Jeremiah's complaints were justified. He was called to speak God's word to God's people, and God's people refused to hear. In a striking image in Jeremiah 52, he had eaten a scroll containing the words of the Lord and had found them 'sweet to the taste'. That memory, however, has now receded, and the people's rejection of his message makes him bitter. God points out that their rejection of the prophet's message is paralleled in their rejection of himself. If Jeremiah could return to a right understanding of his calling, he would understand that people must return to understand the message, to respond to it and so receive mercy. By causing the people to repent, God will requite Jeremiah for all that he has suffered. Psalm 26 echoes the theme of the prophet's faithfulness. Like Jeremiah, he has kept himself free from all entanglement with the enemies of God; he is therefore convinced of his eventual vindication.

St Paul's teaching in Romans 12 continues his exposition of the paradoxical 'living sacrifice' of Romans 12:1. The practical details of what he urges are worthy of serious attempt; their very specificity constitutes a challenge!

The second half of Matthew 16 balances the first half. In 1:15 Peter is the great example of faith, insight and commitment; so much

Application

Disciples of Jesus are called to set their minds on divine things – the cross and the path to glory. 'Human things' are avoidance of pain and the search for easy paths of discipleship. Such a search is vain, for such paths do not exist; only those who make a conscious effort to 'deny themselves', that is, not seek their own interests first, are worthy to follow in the footsteps of Jesus. The rewards for this are in the sphere of the kingdom of God, not in earthly or material gain.

so that he is called 'The Rock', upon which Jesus will build his chosen community. Here Peter is Satan, suggesting that there are ways to salvation and glory other than by the way of the cross.

The final sentence rightly belongs with the next paragraph in the Gospel; its link is with the notion of the Son of Man coming in his kingdom; that promise is fulfilled in the story of the Transfiguration.

Ordinary Time – Proper 18

Sunday between 4 and 10 September

Exodus 12:1–14 *with* Psalm 149; *or* Ezekiel 33:7–11 *with* Psalm 119:33–40; Romans 13:8–14; Matthew 18:15–20

According to Passover tradition the youngest son asks his father, 'Why is this night different from all other nights?' and is then instructed to celebrate the meal as if he and his family had just come out of Egypt, 'out of bondage to freedom, from sorrow to gladness, and from mourning to festival day, from darkness to great light, and from servitude to redemption' (Pesach 10:5). What is described in today's Exodus passage is a family celebration, with a sacred meal that did not need priest or altar. It is this domestic practice which was almost certainly revived during Israel's exile in Babylon. The exodus represented the birth of the nation, so the keeping of Passover was vital to her survival as the People of God and could not be abandoned for lack of the temple cult.

Matthew, like the exilic scribes responsible for editing Exodus, wants to establish new ways for his diverse group to establish an identity. The chapter from which our Gospel reading comes is concerned with church order. It may well be addressed to Christian leaders. No one is to have special rank or status in the household of faith, they are to make a place for the alienated and embody a method of communal correction. They are to be aware that prayer is a shared activity: there are to be no professional mediators between God and his people when Jesus is in the midst. The passage might imply that Matthew's church was already an egalitarian bunch, though some evidence suggests otherwise. Clearly, however, he expects his call to be a new community of inclusive love and energizing forgiveness to be realised. It is not an ideal beyond reach. He is aware of the dangers inherent in his church's adherence to Law and authority, and has built in some correctives. He knows well enough that there is authority exercised in the church; but in itself such authority is neither Christian nor unchristian. That will depend on the way it is exercised and on a reluctance to appeal to it.

Adherence to Law and authority offers something of a thread between today's readings. Paul, having tackled the question of the 'governing authorities', now returns to conclude his section on Christian behaviour with the all-inclusive 'Law of love'. Just as Roman rule guaranteed some stability until Jesus's return, so there is an onus on Christians to 'wake from sleep' and live the new life which they have already 'put on' in baptism.

Ezekiel (the related reading) is concerned with the prophet's commission to be a moral sentinel to warn the people to turn back from their evil ways, a responsibility which went with his powers of far-sightedness. This is less about warning the whole people of God's punishment than it is about erring individuals – who must be confronted personally. The prophet, like Matthew, knows that in most groups the tendency is not to go directly to whoever is causing

Application

Matthew's Gospel shows an interest in the responsibility incumbent on individuals to stand against the prevailing order. Notice particularly his treatment of the Passion narrative. And, at the Jewish Passover, each one present considers themselves as if they had personally come out of Egypt. Freedom was not lightly won and is not without remembrance in every generation. There are two kinds of slavery: a physical enslavement and a spiritual slavery, expressed by the worship of idols (Joshua 24:2). At Passover both have to be addressed. The 'gods of Pharaoh' must also be defeated in the struggle for liberation. Human beings have always found ways to misuse religion, as often as not to create their own new kinds of slavery. The holiest place or tradition of one generation can become an idol for the next. The god we can define is no longer God. The opposite of liberation and freedom is ultimately idolatry. We are each of us duty-bound to seek out and destroy the idols that enslave us.

'Blessed are You, our Living God, Sovereign of the universe, who has not made me a slave!'

(from the Shema)

trouble, but to go over their head to someone with **real** power. Both are summoning us to take our own share of responsibility for the ordering of Church and world. A short section from Psalm 119 enables us to respond positively in the prayer that God's statutes be written in our hearts and lives.

Ordinary Time – Proper 19

Sunday between 11 and 17 September

Exodus 14:19–31 *with either* Psalm 114 *or* Exodus 15:1b–11,
20–21; *or* Genesis 50:15–21 *with* Psalm 103:1–7 *or* 1–13;
Romans 14:1–12; Matthew 18:21–35

Somehow forgiveness is always simpler to urge on others than it is
to offer on our own behalf. If we have not received the forgiveness
given to us, we shall not easily pass it on, and in this final reading
from Matthew 18 – the chapter on church order – Jesus's concern is
with constant forgiveness. He illustrates his point with the parable of
the servant who received totally gracious cancellation of an immense
debt (even King Herod only had an annual income of 900 talents, so
10,000 is 'billions' in our terms) only to refuse a fellow servant forgiveness of a minor debt. This is advice on pastoral care within the
community. For Matthew, church order is about the authority and
freedom to forgive – not about the withholding of forgiveness. His
intention is always to prevent the abuse of power in the Church, so
that the message of Jesus may be clearly heard.

Paul too is dealing with issues of church order, and his conclusions
are remarkably similar. He is making special reference to a particular
food-related problem which may well divide Jewish and Gentile
Christians. His advice will serve us all well in areas where we are
divided. Both groups are to avoid disparaging each other's views.
One may well be right – but neither is in a position to condemn the
other. Only God can do that – and the message is that all live by faith
in the light of his forgiveness and in anticipation of his mercy.

The crossing of the Red Sea is the event to which the people of
Israel will always look back as the sign and promise of God's faith-
fulness and loving-kindness. For Christians it prefigures the work of
Jesus in cancelling the power of sin – and throughout history it has
inspired innumerable oppressed groups in their quest for freedom. In
this context it is a salutary reminder, in anticipation of Paul and
Matthew, that God's people owe a loyalty to human liberation
beyond anything they owe to religious institutions. The choice of
Canticle is between Psalm 114, a Passover hymn in celebration of
God's presence and power, and the Song of Thanksgiving from

Exodus 15, which is the most ancient written record we have of the deliverance from the Egyptians.

The alternative Old Testament reading is the story of Joseph forgiving his brothers at the end of the book of Genesis. They come and throw themselves upon his mercy and so fulfil the dream (of their bowing down before him) with which the whole story began. Like all the stories in Genesis this is more than just a tidy ending to an historical account. It is also related to present and future and the mutual forgiveness to which God's people are summoned. For this writer, as for Paul, 'all things work together for good', and the Psalm 'Bless the Lord, O my soul' is a fitting response with which to glorify God, 'as far as the morning is from the evening, so far does he remove our transgressions from us. As a father has compassion on his children, so the Lord has compassion on those who fear him.'

Application

How do we live with difference within the body of Christ? Division and schism have already occurred, and more divisions and schisms are likely, for the problems will not quickly be resolved. Can we seek the grace of God and display the transformative reality of Christ in our midst? Have we genuinely listened to what our neighbour, with whom we disagree, is saying, so that we can speak wisely and truly to their condition? Fudging the issue is never a solution. But we live in a tension between present and future: the birth-pangs are inevitable.

Ordinary Time – Proper 20

Sunday between 18 and 24 September

Exodus 16:2–15 *with* Psalm 105:1–6, 37–45; *or* Jonah 3:10–4.11
with Psalm 145:1–8; Philippians 1:21–30; Matthew 20:1–16

Faith in God begins from his loving initiative. There are no conditions attached: our first and only duty is to accept his care and
delight. Mutual self-giving may be the appropriate response, but it is
never wrested from us. The story of manna in the wilderness, which
follows on from the crossing of the Red Sea, is about trusting the gift.
Last week's narrative came as the climax to all the sufferings in
Egypt, with the recognition by both Israelites and Egyptians that the
Lord is indeed God. This week we move on to the people's difficulty
in making this act of faith a reality. Today's story serves first to illustrate the nature of God's providence: 'this is the bread which the
Lord has given you to eat', and also to affirm the authority given to
Moses. The Canticle, from Psalm 105, is a hymn of praise which
continues to celebrate in the present God's gifts and promises, which
always precede any demand made upon us.

In contrast to readings from the letter to the Roman Christians
(whom Paul had not yet met) we now move to the letter to the
Philippians, a church for whom he has a warm affection and sympathy – and which seems to be facing opposition. Its main theme therefore is persistence in faith despite tough times. He offers himself as an
example of courage and joy – and reminds them that standing faith-
fully for the gospel, united in what they know to be right, is the privilege of suffering for Christ. It is a privilege, given by God, which
they share with him.

The parable of the labourers in the vineyard tells much the same
story as we have already seen in Matthew. For Jesus the kingdom is
offered to all, whatever their past record, who will by repentance
receive it. This is the heart of the gospel – and the implication for
Matthew's community, and for our own, is that there are no grades
of discipleship. All are on an equal footing before God: *'many who
are last will be first, and the first last.'* This is the clear teaching of the
Beatitudes repeated here in dramatic form and with overtones of the
last judgement.

The related Old Testament reading is from the Book of Jonah, the story of Jonah's anger with the Lord for not punishing the people of Nineveh – and his theological debate with God about God's qualities! Nineveh is saved because of God's patience, which also extends to Jonah, the reluctant prophet. We don't know whether he had a change of heart. We want to think he did. God challenges Jonah, in the same way as Jesus challenges the disciples, to be unstintingly generous. Paul too wants the Philippians to be towards each other as he is towards them. There is a mutual self-offering towards which the readings point us, but always God's patience and our freedom extend beyond the pages of the book.

Text

The story of Jonah – the prophet of the great fish – has captured the imagination of artists everywhere. It is not the sole property of Jews or Christians – or indeed Muslims – though Jonah is a favourite subject in Islamic legend. It is essentially a story designed to be heard. Much of it is in direct discourse, so the storyteller can take the role of the characters. There is lots of repetition: the **greatness** (14 times) of the fish, the storm, the fear, the city (4:11), the **gladness** (4:6). James Limburg (*Jonah*, SCM, 1993) focuses attention on the fourteen questions of this short book. The eight questions directed at Jonah by the Captain and sailors in chapter 1 serve to put the listener into Jonah's shoes. Then Jonah asks a question of the Lord (2:4), the king of Nineveh asks a rhetorical question (3:9), and in the final chapter, set for today's reading, Jonah puts an angry question to the Lord (4:2) and God addresses three questions to Jonah (4:4, 9, 11). The listeners are left with the final question, 'Should I not be concerned about Nineveh . . . ?', ringing in their ears and addressed personally to each of them. The story invites both the people of God and the peoples of the world to join in with the song of praise emerging from the belly of the great fish.

Ordinary Time – Proper 21

Sunday between 25 September and 1 October

Exodus 17:1–7 *with* Psalm 78:1–4, 12–16; *or* Ezekiel 18:1–4, 25–32
with Psalm 25:1–9; Philippians 2:1–13; Matthew 21:23–32

The call of today's Ezekiel reading, 'Turn, then, and live', is a salutary reminder that our faith calls us to 'get a life', rather than a religion or a satisfactory creed. The New Testament passages show us the compelling power of Jesus's message – its ability both to turn people around and to provoke them to murderous anger.

The hymn in Philippians is a marvellous example of the early recognition that Jesus somehow embodied the mystery of all life, that through him we know what God is like. In this familiar passage the Christians in Philippi are to stand together against opposition by being 'of one mind' and imitating Christ Jesus. What this means in practice is worked out through the example. The model of reversed values, and of the humble one exalted, is advanced elsewhere by Paul in relation to Christian ministry. Here it serves the cause of church unity.

The Gospel is also concerned with Jesus's reversed values, which seem to provoke such fierce opposition from religious leaders. In the first of a series of confrontations Jesus counters their challenge with the parable of the two sons. Matthew gives us, through this, a caricature of Jewish leadership and a reminder that everything hinges on a gift given in the present moment – rather than on rules created by precedent. It is a story, unique to Matthew, which could be directly applied to the specifics of his own situation. However, it also has more general application. As always in this Gospel Christian belief is about faithful discipleship, about actions which speak louder than words. This is the first of a trilogy of polemical and very Matthaean parables. The gulf between Jesus and the leaders has become steadily wider. The double confession of Jesus as 'Son of David' has sparked off bitter dispute, and we seem to be in contact with the arrogant claims of religious people whenever they 'know best'. Elsewhere in the Gospel Matthew sets out a portrait of the Davidic messiah which differs markedly from current expectations. Jesus is the one who is 'meek and lowly in heart' (11:29), the 'humble king' (21:5). In this emphasis he is developing a theme found in earlier Christian traditions, and he contrasts the humility and meekness of Jesus, Son of David, with the glory of his future coming as Son of Man. He is encouraging his own readers to be ready for that coming – while at the same time reflecting in their own lives, just like the Christians at Philippi, the humble servant of God confronted at every turn by opponents.

The continuous Old Testament reading is about the people's grumbling at the privations of the desert: 'Why did you bring us out of Egypt to kill us?', and about Moses striking water from the rock at God's bidding. The strange and threatening conditions are very different of course from those suffered by the Philippian Christians and by Matthew's community, but the message of God's providence is the same. Verses from Psalm 78, set as the Canticle, portray the

Application

The Ezekiel reading reinforces this Gospel's focus on God's will to save. The prophet is announcing a new beginning following the judgement of the Exile. It is a beginning based on individual conscience and responsibility. The idea of collective responsibility and punishment was widespread in ancient times, and the individual was unimportant compared with the community. The proverb at Ezekiel 18:2 challenges the justice of God's punishment, and the prophet is commissioned to reply to an assault on the righteousness of God. It is God's prerogative to judge each individual according to his or her responsibility, he says, but he is also commenting on a social crisis in a way that opens the path for universal salvation. The New Testament message similarly is not confined to God and an individual or a chosen group; the people of God are to recognize their solidarity with all humanity. The goal is still ahead of us; we are all on a journey from the present world into one to come. God's salvation is unlimited.

irrational quality of past events, 'riddles from of old', so that God's people may never forget that they owe their survival to divine guidance and help.

The alternative reading comes from the prophet Ezekiel and is concerned with an individual responsibility and change of heart required of everyone. It relates closely to the Matthaean call to the Jewish leaders, who failed to respond to the preaching of John the Baptist and thereby sealed their own fate. Because tax collectors and prostitutes received that preaching, they are closer to the Kingdom than the religious professionals. The personal petition of Psalm 25 makes the appropriate response: the Psalmist is conscious that trust in God is the only hope not to be 'put to shame'. Moral rectitude is not so much an accomplishment as the gift of divine grace.

Ordinary Time – Proper 22

Sunday between 2 and 8 October

Exodus 20:1–4, 7–9, 12–20 *with* Psalm 19; *or* Isaiah 5:1–7 *with* Psalm 80:7–15; Philippians 3.4b–14; Matthew 21:33–46

The image of setting out towards a goal, by way of suffering, makes a connection between the intense confrontations described by Matthew, and Paul's message to the Philippians. The parable of the vineyard and the tenants recalls the opening of Isaiah's song of the vineyard in the related reading. Both are about the failure of God's people to live by the covenant. The fate which will shortly befall Jesus is predicted, and the blame for it laid on the Jewish leaders. God hands 'Israel' over to others, who show the fruit of good works. This forms a logical sequel to the story of the two sons, its main thrust going to the more general matter of rejection of Jesus's authority by all those who resist grace in favour of some system of divine legalism and retribution.

The Philippians passage explicitly picks up some of the language of the hymn of chapter 2. Paul allows the form of Christ's self-emptying to be the form of his own existence. Unlike those who preach circumcision, he does not cling to a status of which he can boast, but receives the gift of righteousness that comes by faith. So also should the Philippians. The process has not yet been completed in Paul; he still must struggle as an athlete (vv. 12–14). He has not reached the resurrection glory, but is still being conformed to the suffering of Christ. This is their call as well, since 'Christ Jesus has made them his own.' Like Jesus, in conflict with the Jewish leaders, they too are setting out towards a goal. Suffering is still in sight, but their acceptance in the gospel is unearned and this is cause for surpassing joy.

The Old Testament reading, from Exodus, is the giving of the Ten Commandments – recalling the making of the Sinai covenant and bringing all of life under an obligation to God. These are not strictly Laws so much as a description of what is expected of God's covenant people, how all the most basic demands of moral life in society are related to him. They are addressed directly to the individual in the second person singular, but relate to actions with a strongly corporate character. Psalm 19 brings together two hymns, the first in praise of creation and the second in praise of the Law of the Lord, so making the connection between the gift of life and the covenant by which that life is maintained. It then moves to a prayer in praise of the blessings of inner happiness and joy which result.

Deep down many of us prefer to rely on our own independent resources than to accept God's freely given love. This shows itself in ways that are all too familiar: our dependence on work, possessions and compulsions, our ruthless competitiveness. The parable from Isaiah spells out the inevitable consequences of this loss of vision in our affairs: injustice, oppression and bloodshed. The Canticle repeats it in the form of an ancient prayer of repentance, calling on God to return and revisit his people. All in the end is the gift of grace.

Text

The Jews marked Pentecost with a twenty-four-hour vigil, designed to remember Moses at Sinai and to extol the wonders of the Law. In the synagogue the main focus was on the Ten Commandments (or 'Ten Words' in Judaism) which opened the Mosaic code. In Matthew's Gospel can it be coincidental that the first uninterrupted teaching portrays Jesus on a mountain giving a new version of the Torah? Jesus relives, for this Evangelist, the life experiences of Moses during forty days in the wilderness. And in the Sermon on the Mount, Jesus is the New Moses, recalling the rich young man to the commandments (Matthew 19:16–22) and, in this parable, reminding us that Moses too was in danger of being stoned by those who would not accept his message. Matthew's respect for the law of the Jews was deeply held. To Mark's text he added the words that not 'one letter, not one stroke of a letter' will pass from the law 'until all is accomplished' (Matthew 5:18). For Matthew the law pointed to Christ and it has been suggested that his Gospel was designed to be read against the background of the Jewish liturgical year (see Michael Goulder *Midrash and Lection in Matthew*, SPCK, 1974). If so, it is less a biography of Jesus than a profound interpretation of what his life teaches about the God of Israel and of Moses.

Ordinary Time – Proper 23

Sunday between 9 and 15 October

Exodus 32:1–14 *with* Psalm 106:1–6, 19–23; *or* Isaiah 25:1–9 *with* Psalm 23; Philippians 4:1–9; Matthew 22:1–14

The parable of the wedding banquet is more savage than the story of the vineyard in its judgement on unfaithful Israel. Yet even here grace is sovereign. It needs to be set in the context of the marriage supper of the Lamb in Revelation 19, the climactic scriptural image. It then carries all the festive overtones of the marriage feast at Cana, the Last Supper, the breaking of bread on the road to Emmaus and the breakfast by the lakeside – not to mention Passover. All are summoned to a party, but the sad truth is that the invitation is not heard or heeded. We want our merits rewarded – and others to get their deserts. We too have other plans.

Three powerful parables have each condemned the Jewish leadership for their opposition to God's purposes: the failure to repent, the failure to live by the covenant and, here, the failure to heed God's repeated invitations to take part in the kingdom. By opposition to Jesus and his message the religious leaders have shown themselves in opposition to God the Father. We too need to hear the warnings. We are only saved by the acceptance of an invitation.

Our readings from Philippians are coming to an end, and in this passage the warmth of Paul's relationship with his readers comes through forcefully. Some of the mission workers are not getting along, and the false teachers are fomenting dissension, but there is a quality of joy and affection which counters everything else. Paul has made equality, unity and friendship the organizing principles of the letter. His own self-assertiveness has been kept in check while he turns to the task of proclaiming the gospel in the face of suffering, aiming to follow the 'mind' of Christ.

The story of the golden calf represents a reflection on a pagan element in Israel's worship. It is set as the sequel to the Law-giving on Sinai, and this reinforces the awful disloyalty such apostasy reflects, and the readiness to resort back to Canaanite practice. It is a lesson against the kind of worship which has recurred at many times in the history of God's people, warning us all that worship of the

One God is not mediated by way of lesser 'idols', however worthy. Like those invited to the banquet we may not choose our own path in defiance of God. The Canticle seems to have originated in the autumn ceremonies of covenant renewal, reflecting on the grace by which God has brought the people back to himself from their many acts of disobedience.

The alternative reading, from Isaiah, is a song of praise for deliverance from oppression. It relates to the parable of the great feast, in describing and celebrating a coronation banquet, a theme that continues into later apocalyptic literature (such as Revelation 19). The triumph of God marks the end of history – with death, the last enemy, finally destroyed. In the New Testament the banquet forms part of the thinking in the presentation of the Lord's Supper (see 1 Corinthians 15:22–27). Psalm 23 offers a word picture of God as the

---

Application
Love

Love bade me welcome; yet my soul drew back,
Guilty of dust and sin.
But quick-eyed Love, observing me grow slack
From my first entrance in,
Drew nearer to me, sweetly questioning,
If I lack anything.

'A guest,' I answered, 'worthy to be here.'
Love said, 'You shall be he.'
'I, the unkind, ungrateful? Ah, my dear,
I cannot look on Thee.'
Love took my hand, and smiling, did reply,
'Who made the eyes but I?'

'Truth, Lord, but I have marred them; let my shame
Go where it doth deserve.'
'And know you not,' says Love, 'who bore the blame?'
'My dear, then I will serve.'
'You must sit down,' says Love, 'and taste my meat.'
So I did sit and eat.

loving host feeding and protecting the individual, as a shepherd protects the sheep. It lies behind the poetry of George Herbert's 'Love bade me welcome' and reminds us that, despite a gospel parable of judgement, grace is always sovereign.

Ordinary Time – Proper 24

Sunday between 16 and 22 October

Exodus 33:12–23 *with* Psalm 99; *or* Isaiah 45:1–7 *with*
Psalm 96:1–9 *or* 1–13; 1 Thessalonians 1:1–10; Matthew 22:15–22

There is an authority issue which underlies all the controversies between Jesus and the Jewish leaders in Matthew. He is perceived as a threat to the continued existence of Jewish society because he places himself above Law and tradition. The confrontation over paying taxes to Caesar probably reflects anxiety about any open disloyalty to Rome, which a refusal to pay might have demonstrated. From Jesus's perspective, there is no threat to true Judaism – the debates about Law and tradition are all to be resolved by the proper application of one basic principle, utter devotion to God and love of neighbour. The implication of the story is that this is the issue which divides him from the religious leaders. They cannot catch him out as a hot-headed radical who is prepared to risk the lives of others. So they resort to the one option they believe is still open to them, and gather to consult on how to bring about his arrest and death. The events of the Passion account itself have already begun.

Paul's first letter to the Thessalonians is the earliest example of Christian literature in the New Testament. It is concerned with the identity of the community and, in order to strengthen their sense of who they are, Paul reminds them of their beginnings. By God's call they have become part of God's people, turning their lives towards the true and living God. Their behaviour must be measured by God's own life, a share of which is given to them by the power of the Holy Spirit. Living by such a measure will involve affliction.

The Old Testament reading is the story of Moses interceding with God at the Tent of Meeting and asking to see his face. It is concerned with God's presence with the Israelites once they have departed from Sinai, the assumption being that this is closely tied to the mountain itself. In the end it is God's word – rather than his visible image – which provides the guarantee that he is with Israel, safeguarding her unique identity as the people of God. For both ancient Israel and the Thessalonian Christians it is God's living and continuing call which establishes and maintains them as a community. The Canticle,

Psalm 99, is an enthronement hymn related to the Covenant Festival – an ancient witness to God's holiness and dominion.

The alternative reading is from the second part of Isaiah, chapters concerned with the end of the Babylonian empire and the rise of Persia under Cyrus. In this passage Cyrus is described as an agent of God's restorative action. The idea of being rescued by a Gentile must have been radical enough to provoke serious resistance – much as Jesus's suggestion, in the Gospel, that God's kingdom would be brought in independently of the Jewish establishment. But Jesus, like Second Isaiah, teaches straight out of the tradition. His parables and answers subvert the oppressive systems much as the poetry of this passage undermines the despair of the exiles. Psalm 96 is another enthronement hymn in which God enters upon his reign over the world. It is a vision which embraces every sphere of life and restores his order in nature and in history.

Application

Paying taxes to the emperor might be construed as disloyalty to the God of Israel. Jesus's reply allowed him to escape the opposite charge of disloyalty to Rome, without really solving the problem! People who wanted to avoid taxation had to become outlaws but, although Matthew's Gospel encourages Christians to face persecution and martyrdom, there is no suggestion that they should separate out from normal society altogether. Most likely there had already been a split between the followers of Jesus and the Jewish synagogue. The anti-Jewish polemic of Matthew 23 is embarrassing to modern Christians: probably Matthew saw Israel's rejection of its Messiah as bringing God's judgement. His community is committed to evangelism, but they are not being very successful . . . so he sets out his view of Jesus's life in the light of accusations and criticisms from elsewhere. He is struggling with the problem of the relationship between two accounts: that of the early followers, on the one hand, and that of their Jewish detractors, on the other.

Ordinary Time – Proper 25

Sunday between 23 and 29 October

Deuteronomy 34:1–12 *with* Psalm 90:1–6, 13–17; *or*
Leviticus 19:1–2, 15–18 *with* Psalm 1; 1 Thessalonians 2:1–8;
Matthew 22:34–46

The confrontation between Jesus and the Jewish leadership continues with a test question about the 'greatest commandment'.
The Pharisees are silenced by an answer with which no Jew could
have found fault, echoing Deuteronomy 6:5 and quoting Leviticus
19:18. Human piety towards God and love of one another remain
the basis of the good life, both Jewish and Christian. The principle is
not in question; from it the Law in all its detailed provision derives.
Here it sums up a sense in which Jesus's teaching is the final interpretation of God's commandments, so it is appropriately placed at the
climax of his dealings with the Jewish teachers, his final positive pro-
nouncement on the subject. The concluding debate happens at the
initiative of Jesus himself, and its position is enhanced by Matthew's
special concern with 'Son of David' as a title for Jesus, one which
particularly provokes Jewish hostility. In Matthew's scheme of things
Jesus's humility made him a better messianic agent of God than even
the great King David.

The reading from 1 Thessalonians is also about 'agency' and
about humility: Paul's sense of his ministry in Thessalonica needing
defence against accusations about his character and motives. He
forcefully asserts his straightforwardness as well as his affectionate
caring for the Thessalonian Christians, like a nurse or a parent.

The Old Testament reading is the final passage at the end of
Deuteronomy, the story of Moses's death and burial in the land
of Moab, and of Joshua taking up the reins. As the primary leader of
the Israelites in their Exodus from Egypt, and as mediator of the
Law, Moses dominates the foundation scriptures of the Jewish and
Christian traditions. Jesus as the New Moses is, in Matthew's
Gospel, the ultimate teacher of the things of God. The Canticle
responds to the problem of the relationship between God and human
beings from the point of view of God's eternal being and the tran-
sience of human nature. It is ascribed to Moses, an old man looking

back on his life, who recapitulates the whole tradition of the 'Books of Moses' right back to creation and fall – and then concludes the Psalm with a prayer for God's help in the light of eternity, contrasted with his frail humanity.

The alternative reading is directly quoted in Jesus's response to the Pharisees about the 'greatest commandment'. First-century Jews commonly summarized the twin aspects of the Law as human piety towards God and love of one another. No one could find fault with Jesus's answer! The alternative Canticle is Psalm 1, deliberately given first place in the Psalter in order to summon the reader to obedience to God's will. It is God's Law which safeguards the faithful Jew's life, enabling the image of God to be reflected in it. The person absorbed in the Law is compared with a green tree full of sap which, planted by a watercourse, bears its fruit in due season.

Background

Christian use of Psalm 110 certainly goes back to Paul (1 Corinthians 15:25). It was much quoted as an explanation for the delay between the exaltation of Jesus and the end of the world. In Hebrews it lies behind 'he sat down at the right hand of the Majesty on high' (Hebrews 1:3) – a privilege reserved for David's descendants. Here, Matthew is emphasizing that Jesus was 'Son of David' – and more than 'Son of David'. The tribe of Judah produced King David and the whole Davidic royal line. The line was then lost in the sixth century BC, thanks to Babylonian defeat, and the idea of a messiah king 'like King David' became part of Israel's hope for the future. This messiah would be of the royal line and therefore from David's tribe of Judah. He had to be born in the city of David's birth, Bethlehem, a tradition that helped to shape Matthew's birth narrative. But it is worth noting that, in this Gospel, acknowledgement of Jesus as 'Son of David' provokes hostility from the Jewish leaders. Matthew is aware of the controversy and seems to be claiming that this title lies at the heart of Christian conviction – although his portrait clearly differs from current expectation: 'your king is humble . . . and mounted on a donkey' (21:5).

Bible Sunday

Nehemiah 8:1–4a *or* 1–6, 8–12; Psalm 119:9–16;
Colossians 3:12–17; Matthew 24:30–35

Bible Sunday will usually be observed on the Last Sunday after Trinity (though this is not mandatory), and the Gospel reading accords well with such a pattern, following on from Jesus's confrontations with the Jewish leadership about how scripture should be interpreted. The Old Testament reading also links neatly to the narratives from Exodus and Deuteronomy. The newly compiled Law is brought back from Babylon, by Ezra, as part of the attempt to establish purity of community and worship in Judah after the Exile. The reading of the book – a version of the Pentateuch – was central to a renewed relationship with God. Nehemiah certainly did not regard the Law as the only form of mediation between humans and God; he believed in immediate contact through prayer. But he also had a strong view of the power of scripture, and insisted that it be interpreted to the people. Since it was in Hebrew, this meant that the more familiar Aramaic was probably used – and this seems to have moved them to repentance.

The Canticle from Psalm 119 focuses on the word of God as the decisive factor in every sphere of life. The Psalmist has been brought low by suffering, and regards the Law as his most precious treasure and as the standard of his conduct in life. There is no sign here of any hardening into the legalism which provoked Jesus's rebuke, but the feeling expressed carries with it the germ of possible development towards self-righteousness. Even God's most treasured gifts become idols when they are made the only arbiters of good behaviour.

The reading from Colossians describes the positive effects of new life in Christ. In a call to 'seek the things that are above' Christians are asked to 'let the word of Christ dwell in you richly', an expression which probably refers to the stories and sayings of Jesus we know from the Gospels. There is something attractive about the idea of being so at home in the gospel story, setting it alongside our experience and making it our own. In a sense the author of Colossians is demonstrating something similar. This passage carries echoes of earlier sections, and applies here to those who belong to

Christ what is there said of him personally. It is in Jesus that Christians find their identity as God's people.

For Matthew too, especially on the eve of the crucifixion, following Jesus is the key to Christian belief. The weightier matters of the Law (23:23) are justice, mercy and faith – and God's people will be devoted to obedience to these ordinances of scripture, as interpreted by Jesus himself. Matthew seems to be concerned that Jesus should not be thought of as the enemy of the Mosaic Law, and for him Jesus has 'not come to abolish the Law or the prophets . . . but to fulfil them.' At the same time it is the word of Jesus which is normative for the Church and which fulfils and supersedes the word of Moses. The Law is to be observed as long as it does not conflict with the Law of love. We see the new Christian community struggling in its relationship with the religion it has broken away from – precisely because devotion to the Bible has become legalistic, and ultimately idolatrous, leading to a self-righteousness which can no longer hear the living word of freedom.

Text

Psalm 119, a hymn of praise to the Torah, is the longest by far in the Psalter. It has been suggested that the Sermon on the Mount was patterned by Matthew on this Psalm, which also begins with the word 'Blessed . . .', in order to fit the Pentecost celebrations of the Jewish liturgy (Goulder, M. D., *Midrash and Lection in Matthew*, SPCK, 1974). Whether or not one takes this view of Matthew 5–7, the Psalm certainly had a liturgical purpose and was divided into twenty-two stanzas, each marked by one of the twenty-two letters of the Hebrew alphabet. (It manages to find words beginning with the same letter for eight successive verses before moving on to the next!) It carries the worshipper through the different sections of a twenty-four-hour watch: 'Seven times a day will I praise you' (Psalm 119:164). 'I remember your name in the night, O Lord' (v. 55), 'At midnight I rise to praise you' (v. 62), 'Oh, how I love your law! It is my meditation all day long' (v. 97), 'I rise before dawn and cry for help' (v. 147), 'My eyes are awake before each watch of the night' (v. 148).

Dedication Festival

First Sunday in October or Last Sunday after Trinity

1 Kings 8:22–30 *or* Revelation 21:9–14; Psalm 122;
Hebrews 12:18–24; Matthew 21:12–16

A Dedication Festival brings us to delight and despair, sometimes simultaneously, in church and Christian faith. On the delight side, there is celebration of shared memories and visions, old friends returning, a nostalgia for heaven and fellowship with the Saints; on the despair side, the fixity of the building, our conservatism and dislike of change, our clinging to legalism, the past and the trappings of power. Scripture, in both the Old Testament and the New, addresses the paradox.

The first reading offers the possibility of a choice between Solomon's prayer of dedication (from Kings) and the vision of the New Jerusalem (from Revelation). Solomon's prayer, in the spirit of Deuteronomy, includes the line: 'will God indeed dwell on the earth?', precisely the riddle with which we too contend. The vision of the New Jerusalem is an attempt to describe a symbolic 'dwelling place'. The bride, into which all earth's splendour is gathered, is a living image of creation and Church finally glorified. It is part of a re-reading of biblical tradition in the light of the death of Jesus – the gap between God's will and earth's obedience has been overcome. Struggling Christian groups are to take heart from this dawning of a new age.

The Canticle is Psalm 122, 'I was glad . . .', which is a hymn followed by a prayer for God's blessing on the holy city. The language of peace and salvation makes a deliberate word play on the name 'Jerusalem'. Peace and harmony pervade the Psalm, and the house of God is the spring of God's salvation.

The author of Hebrews speaks of salvation in terms of coming to Mount Zion, an image of movement and of a pilgrim group travelling together. He makes an appeal to the new covenant mediated by Jesus and urges his readers not to lose confidence in God's promises, but to go forward in faith. In this passage he reminds them of the differences between the two covenants, by contrasting Sinai and Zion. Jesus alone has set foot in the supreme sacred territory, heaven.

Compared with heaven, Mount Sinai – and, by association, all our 'holy places' – is merely 'tangible'. The author addresses his Christian readers as those standing on the very brink of the boundary of heavenly Jerusalem. Jesus has desacralized its holy ground, making access to God open to the people. A new covenant has been inaugurated and there follows a solemn warning of the need to take this seriously.

Finally, Matthew's cleansing of the Temple, in contrast to the other accounts of this story, immediately follows the entry into Jerusalem. 'Cave of robbers' is an allusion to Jeremiah, who criticized people for

Application

'From the borders of the Promised Land, we return to the Creation story and begin again . . . We build our tabernacle for God precisely because it is so tangible, so finite. It is structure, form, clarity . . . it guarantees our identity in the wilderness. It reminds us of where we have been and where we seek to go. Yet it may also become prison, obsession or death.

Whenever the cloud was taken up from over the tabernacle the children of Israel went onward throughout all their journeys (Exodus 40:36).

Each time we take our tabernacle apart, assign the pieces, repair and renew and journey on. We preserve and change. When the cloud moves on we must follow or die in the wilderness.

'For we are a rabble of former slaves, bound to one another, unwillingly on our way to the land of promise. We murmur and squabble, yet together we have built our tabernacle. And together we are watching, reluctant, bewildered, impatient, waiting for the cloud to move on.'
(taken from Jonathan Magonet, *A Rabbi's Bible*, SCM Press, 1991, pp.175–78)

supposing that they could behave unethically and idolatrously and still expect God to save them. This was to treat the Temple of God as if it were a cave of robbers. Jesus's words interpret his actions and we too are warned against deluding ourselves in the false security of church membership without the dedication of our lives. Like the Christians addressed in Hebrews, we are a pilgrim band which remains exiled from our final home. While God gives us glimpses of heaven along the way, we are not there yet. All our religious institutions must be at the service of God's mission.

All Saints' Sunday

Revelation 7:9–17; Psalm 34:1–10; 1 John 3:1–3; Matthew 5:1–12

'The period between All Saints' Day and the First Sunday of Advent is observed as a time to celebrate and reflect upon the reign of Christ in earth and heaven.' So say the Rules for ordering the Calendar. These five Sundays are like the 'Home Base' in baseball, where the Catcher stands, and runs start and finish, and all the big hits are made. The cry 'Jesus is Lord!' is the central New Testament confession of faith (see 1 Corinthians 12:3). And so we come back to Home, having run from base to base through the year, and think about Jesus as King, and prepare to start another circuit in Advent. Thinking rightly about 'the reign of Christ in earth and heaven' will help us to knock the ball clean out of the park and make a 'home run' right round the infield!

On All Saints' Day – one of our nine Principal Festivals – we start this process by celebrating *the panorama of his achievement*. These 'saints' are of course not the official canonized saints, but all the baptized and redeemed people of God. 'Saints' is used here is this biblical sense, God's 'holy ones' (see e.g. Romans 1:7). In Revelation 7 John the prophet sees their vast company, 'a great multitude that no one could count', standing in heaven before the throne of God. They have left suffering behind, and are cleansed by 'the blood of the Lamb', never to hunger or thirst again, with the Lamb to shepherd them, and God himself to wipe away every tear. Now they stand before him with the cry of the saved on their lips (7:10). This picture includes everything: the *need* for salvation (suffering and sin), the *ground* of salvation (the blood of Christ), the *scope* of salvation (the multitude from every nation), the *goal* of salvation (fellowship with God in his presence), the *experience* of salvation (safety on a dangerous road), and the *response* to salvation (adoration).

The point about salvation as 'safety on a dangerous road' is important. Revelation 7:16 quotes from Isaiah 49:10, the promise made to exiles for their long and arduous journey back from Babylon to Jerusalem. So although the saints are *pictured* before the throne, the promise of protection applies to those who have not yet arrived, but are still facing the hazards of the road: in other words, to *us*. The saints pictured in Revelation 7 are not 'the Church in glory', but the saints *of the Beatitudes,* our Gospel reading, those who possess 'the kingdom of heaven' but who at the moment are 'poor in spirit', hungering and thirsting for the fulfilment of God's righteous purposes for the world, persecuted but still seeking to make peace, mourning but still able to show mercy, not accepting the world's values but living by Another Star, because they know that 'great is your reward in heaven' (5:12). In their weakness they are *safe,* because they know that 'they will see God' (5:8).

This is all down to the Lordship of Jesus Christ! He is the one who has the *authority* to reverse the values of the world in this way – so

Application

One of C. S. Lewis's most compelling books is *The Great Divorce*. In this the author joins a bus party from hell to heaven, and thus meets some of the inhabitants of both places. In one of these encounters he sees a procession approaching, with dancers and musicians surrounding a mighty lady, shining with joy and beauty. It turns out that she was a housewife from Golders Green called Sarah Smith, who had no children and a shaky marriage to an ineffectual man called Frank, and who died a lonely death in a nursing home . . . but all her life made the lives of others brighter by the love that spilled out of her. Now, says George MacDonald, the heavenly Guide, 'She is one of the great ones. Ye have heard that fame in this country and fame on Earth are two quite different things.' After a moving encounter between herself and Frank, who refuses to accept the new Love in which she lives, she moves away, surrounded by a powerful hymn of praise from the Bright Spirits who accompany her . . . (see C. S. Lewis, *The Great Divorce*, Fount, 1977, pp. 97–110).

This is 'the hope of glory', which according to St Paul is simply 'Christ in you' (Colossians 1:27). Wherever we are, whatever we face, the Lord Christ can turn the grey to gold, let music burst out and love dance between us.

that 'the saints' are not the high achievers, who gain entry to heaven because of their spectacular holiness, but the *poor*, those who know they have nothing to present, but simply hold on to him and live their lives 'on my account' (Matthew 5:11). In their hearts the hope burns bright: 'when he appears, we shall be like him, for we shall see him as he is!' (1 John 3:2).

Text

The Beatitudes – blessings or requirements?

Experts debate what kind of text these sayings are. Some draw a parallel between Jesus on this mountain (Matthew 5:1) and Moses on Mount Sinai, and suggest that the (nine) Beatitudes are the equivalent of the (ten) commandments, giving essential instruction for the disciples of Jesus on how they should live. It is certainly true that in the opening chapters of Matthew's Gospel, Jesus re-runs the history of Israel, going down to Egypt and coming out again, crossing the Red Sea (his baptism) and facing temptations in the wilderness, and it fits that he now arrives on a mountain and we hear 'words' like the 'ten words' that God spoke through Moses.

Others, however, point to the difference in form between these 'words' and the commandments: these are 'beatitudes', that is, pronouncements of blessing on certain types of people. They are not a list of 'entrance requirements' posted for outsiders who might want to enter the Kingdom, but joyfully celebrate for insiders the 'eschatological blessings' that are already theirs.

This second view is probably correct. But the first has some truth in it – not least in allowing us to say how striking it is that, just where we might expect a list of 'rules for life in the Kingdom' parallel to the Ten Commandments, what we get is a glad expression of 'blessedness'. Life in the Kingdom of God is not regulated by rules, but revolves around a relationship with the King, who promises to share his Kingdom with the poor, the hungry, the merciful, the pure in heart, the persecuted. Such promises are inevitably also encouragements to be these things, but the emphasis falls on the 'blessedness'.

The Fourth Sunday before Advent

Sunday between 30 October and 5 November

Micah 3:5–12; Psalm 43; 1 Thessalonians 2:9–13; Matthew 24:1–14

In these Sundays before Advent we undertake consecutive readings from Matthew 24–25: today, the opening section of Matthew 24, and then Matthew 25 in three sections. This long discourse of Jesus focuses on the future, on the 'coming of the Son of Man', and thus helps us to prepare for Advent. Alongside Matthew we read passages from 1 Thessalonians in which Paul answers some concerns about the 'second coming' of Christ, and in doing so draws upon the teaching of Jesus recorded in this part of Matthew.

The 'Kingdom of God' does not arrive easily on planet earth. And for us, the Kingdom of God has become equated with the reign of Christ. So 'the good news of the Kingdom' which must be proclaimed throughout the world (Matthew 24:14) is the *Christian Gospel*, the good news that Jesus is Lord and will save all who call on him. But it is not always 'good news'. Paul 'urges, encourages and pleads' with the Thessalonians to bring their lives into line with the requirements of the Kingdom (1 Thessalonians 2:12; NRSV) – it is clearly not easy for them! Even more 'uneasy' is the message of Matthew 24 itself. The arrival of the Kingdom of God ultimately means the *overthrow* of all other kingdoms, even the kingdom of Israel centred in Jerusalem. If all other kings refuse to yield up their crowns to the King of Kings, then finally they will have them taken away. This is the awesome message of Matthew 24 (the whole chapter, not just verses 1–14).

The Kingdom thus has a rough edge to it. It is not all Good News. Micah warns against false prophets who proclaim peace because that is what people want to hear. Instead, like Jesus, Micah announces the coming destruction of Jerusalem, because of the wickedness of Israel and particularly of her leaders. The Temple about which Micah prophesied was the one built by Solomon, which was eventually destroyed by the Babylonians in 587 BC. Jesus – with great sadness – predicted the destruction of the beautiful building in front of him, the great Temple which Herod the Great had started to build in 19 BC, nearly fifty years earlier, and which was not finished until six years before its complete destruction by the Romans in AD 70. Jesus's prophecy, like Micah's, was fulfilled amid dreadful suffering.

We live in a confused, tumultuous world. Matthew 24:7 speaks of *nations* rising against each other (war based on race and culture), and *kingdoms* fighting (war based on politics, land and economics). These

---

Text

Jesus's 'mini-apocalypse'
Matthew 24 is close in content to Mark 13, and quite close to Luke 21, and together these unusual chapters have been called 'the mini-apocalypse'. We find nothing like this elsewhere on Jesus's lips.

Older scholarship used to question the authenticity of this teaching, on the grounds that it was more likely to have arisen in the early Church after the event predicted, namely the destruction of Jerusalem in AD 70. But readiness to ascribe it to Jesus has grown, on the grounds that (a) it does not contain the kind of literal description of the destruction which we might expect, had it already happened, (b) elements of the material have clearly influenced Paul in 1 and 2 Thessalonians, and therefore must predate those letters, and (c) it is highly likely that Jesus foresaw coming judgement for Israel, when we consider his assessment of the spiritual state of the nation.

Jesus gives his analysis of this in the preceding chapter, Matthew 23. It is in his contemporaries' reaction to himself that he chiefly discerns their disastrous slide towards catastrophe, but also (like Micah) in the pretentiousness, inconsistency and lack of mercy shown by many of their leaders. He speaks with passion and clarity against the rot. Jesus's aim was the same as Micah's: to warn, so as to enable people to prepare, and to escape.

There is some evidence that the 'mini-apocalypse' circulated separately before it was incorporated into Mark's Gospel and then Matthew's, perhaps because Christians wanted to spread the warning to their fellow Jews. Interestingly, Josephus, the Jewish historian, tells us of another Jesus who haunted the streets of Jerusalem in the early 60s AD, simply warning over and over again of the coming destruction. People laughed at him.

---

first-century words have an ominously twentieth-century ring. But the people of the Christ must not be 'alarmed', because they have confidence in a Sovereign whose purpose cannot be thwarted. 'All this *must* take place, but the end is not yet' (24:6). And yet the people of the Christ are caught up in all the turmoil, and may have to face great suffering themselves before the End comes (24:9–10, amplified later in the chapter). We are not exempted. In the midst of the struggle, we are called to 'lead a life worthy of God, who calls you into his own Kingdom and glory' (1 Thessalonians 2:12): with eyes fixed on the future Kingdom, we shape our lives in the present, confident in the King.

Application

Should Christian leaders today seek to speak prophetically, like Jesus and Micah? Genuine prophetic insight is rare, and it is easy to dress up political preferences as prophecy. That is actually what Micah attacks, so we must be warned. But we may still seek from God the ability to see beneath the surface, to discern the spirit of our age and its direction, and to warn of the consequences. We may not be able to make specific prophecies, like Micah and Jesus, but if we are wise we can still speak in God's name.

The Third Sunday before Advent

Sunday between 6 and 12 November

Wisdom of Solomon 6:12–16 *with* Wisdom of Solomon 6:17–20;
or Amos 5:18–24 *with* Psalm 70; 1 Thessalonians 4:13–18;
Matthew 25:1–13

Matthew 25 contains three stories, all looking forward to 'the coming of the Son of Man' (Matthew 24:44). These stories form our Gospel readings for the next three Sundays, directing our thoughts in different ways towards the Lordship and reign of Christ.

The theme that unites these stories is *judgement:* not a theme that sits well in our anti-authoritarian, post-modern culture. Our culture prizes *individual judgement* – in fact, we instil it into our children from the very start of their school careers. Our whole educational ethos rests on the value that children must be taught to think for themselves, to learn how to direct their own learning, to become autonomous, confident human beings. Fine: but we then of course object when they rebel against teachers and parents alike, and choose

---

Background

The wedding and the bridesmaids
The scene is a village wedding, with a group of servant-girls waiting for the bridegroom to return home, with the bride, from the main wedding celebration. They have planned a party to welcome them, and have made lamps – probably bits of rag tied on sticks. Dipped in oil, these would burn for a while, but would frequently need to be re-dipped. The five 'wise' girls have realised this, and have bought extra oil. The 'foolish' ones think of it just in time to dash off to a neighbour to get some more. But the happy couple arrive while they are gone, and when they get back they find to their amazement that the bridegroom will not let them in!

---

fun and friends over sense and schooling. We never meant it to go that far! But we sowed the seeds ourselves, when we gave up *for ourselves* the belief that, ultimately, we have to render account for our lives to Someone Else who will say, 'Think *for yourselves?* Rather, you should have thought *for me!*'

Part of believing in the 'reign of Christ' is that he becomes the final reference point of our existence. And that is what we mean when we confess that he will 'come to judge the living and the dead.' Ultimately, all life finds its reference point in the *judgement* of Christ, that is, in his *mind* about its quality (or not). The dead too, says Paul, will rise to meet Christ. His Lordship extends over all humanity. And this is where the *reading of scripture* becomes so vital a feature of our worship: for, if we are ready to confess him as 'judge of the living and the dead', then we need to hear his mind *now,* so as to be ready to stand before him *then.*

The parable of the 'wise and foolish bridesmaids' is against *presumption.* It must have been told initially with a chuckle but with a sudden silence at the end, when we reach the extraordinary and unexpected v. 12. There the laughter ceases. Jesus's parables often have an element in them that breaks the bounds of the credible: like a mustard plant that can accommodate birds' nests, or a woman who uses a whole barrel of flour to make bread (Matthew 13:31–33). It is usually this unexpected element which carries the main point of the parable, for it makes people sit up and take notice. Here, it is quite inconceivable that a groom would not let his own servant girls into the house. Why does he lock them out? And also say that he does not know them?

Our Old Testament reading points to the answer. There Amos announces a similar surprise. Some people have been looking forward to 'the day of the Lord', because they think it will mean victory, peace and prosperity at last. But No! says Amos: 'that day will be darkness, not light' (v. 18). The God whom they trusted to vindicate and prosper them will turn out to be their *enemy.*

Jesus had already made exactly this point to his own followers, when he referred to those who call him 'Lord, Lord' but do not do his Father's will (Matthew 7:21). Whatever their qualifications in spirituality, when they knock on the door of the Kingdom he will say, 'I never knew you; go away from me, you evildoers' (7:23). We cannot *presume* entry on the basis of *our* assessment of our spiritual worth or standing. *He* is the Judge.

What do we need? Of course, wisdom – the quality of the other girls, celebrated in the alternative Old Testament reading. What is wisdom? It is equipping ourselves to meet the King, and we discover how to do this in the other two stories in Matthew 25.

Text /Theology

Paul's understanding of the second coming of Christ is illuminated by two of the words he uses in 1 Thessalonians 4. The word *parousia* in 4:15, usually translated 'coming', suggests a royal visitation – the 'presence' of the King who has a right to visit any part of his realm. So, although Paul believed in the presence of Christ in the Church by his Spirit, he clearly expected a particular, immediate 'coming' of Christ as King, analogous to the arrival of an emperor. When this King comes, even the dead rise to greet him.

This fits with the rather unusual expression 'meeting' in 4:17. Literally translated: 'we . . . who are left will be caught up with them in the clouds to a meeting with the Lord.' This word 'meeting' has a semi-technical meaning: it was the natural word to use when a group of leading citizens went out from their town to meet with and greet a visiting dignitary, in order to accompany the visitor on the last stages of the journey into the town. It is used, for instance, in Acts 28:15, where the Christians in Rome go out to meet Paul at Three Taverns on the road from Puteoli. So 'meeting the Lord in the clouds / in the air' is not the preliminary to going to heaven with him, but to returning to earth with the King, who now arrives to take up his reign.

Paul thus thought rather literally about the *parousia* of Christ. He transfers to Jesus common Jewish expectations about the coming of the Lord to Zion – although interestingly he does not specify that Jesus will come again at Jerusalem. Somehow, in 1 Thessalonians 4, he thinks of Jesus as returning to earth and in some way being present to 'us', that is, to all believers still alive at the time. Today, many theologians feel a little uncomfortable about Paul's literalism, and prefer to speak of the reign of Christ in terms of his 'ultimacy', or of his 'spiritual supremacy'. But in Paul's ears this would sound like dualism – a distinction between the physical and the spiritual which he did not accept, not least because of the Incarnation. Christ saves us not just as spirits, but as bodies, too – and thus he saves the world in its physical substance, that which he created and over which he reigns as King.

Paul's interpretation of the *parousia* is thus not just a primitive literalism, but arises from his instinctive opposition to dualism: we are physical creatures, so we need a Saviour who embraces our physicality, and who will one day grasp again the stuff of our world and re-assert his rule over it!

The Second Sunday before Advent

Sunday between 13 and 19 November

Zephaniah 1:7, 12–18; Psalm 90:1–8, 12 *or* 1–12;
1 Thessalonians 5:1–11; Matthew 25:14–30

Today's readings continue the exploration of *the reign of Christ* by asking: how should we live under the lordship of Christ? This question is asked and answered at many other points during the year, also: but here we are taken back to 'home base', to first principles, and told that calling Christ 'Lord' means *living in relationship with him, under responsibility, in loving service.*

Zephaniah starts us off with his horrifying portrayal of the coming 'day of the Lord': a frightful picture of unrelieved distress under God's wrath, 'because they have sinned against the Lord' (v. 17). We cannot dismiss this picture as typical of the Old Testament, and call it unworthy of the God whom we worship as the God and Father of Our Lord Jesus Christ, for we meet the same sense of the awful reality of God's final judgement in both our New Testament readings, too – except that here *Christ* is cast in the role of the Judge, as the bringer of 'sudden destruction' to all who trust in a false 'peace and security' without reference to him (1 Thessalonians 5:3). Jesus himself, in the parable of the talents, pictures God as a hard master, who is ready to throw his 'worthless servant' out into the darkness, 'where there will be weeping and gnashing of teeth' (vv. 24, 30).

Is this a *worthy* picture of God, and of Christ? Many Christians feel uncomfortable about it, both because it feels a little fanatical and also because it does not seem to fit well with belief in God's mercy and love. There are important and wider issues involved here, but it is worth asking why the apostle Paul, and Our Lord Jesus, retained this very firm belief in the judgement of God when, at the same time, they emphasized his fatherhood, love and mercy so strongly.

The answer is clear: at rock bottom, God regards our moral choices with the utmost seriousness. He treats us as responsible beings, with the capacity to determine our ultimate relationship with him, by the choices we make now. Finally we undermine our own significance, if we say that it does not matter whether we do good or evil.

What was the difference between the three servants in Jesus's parable? They had different abilities, and thus were given different tasks. The first two achieved different results, but they were treated exactly the same by their returning Lord, because he judged them not by their results but by the quality of their service: 'Well done, good and faithful servant,' he says to them both. So it was not the lack of achievement which displeased the master in the third case, but the lack of love. The servant had not wanted to do his best for his master – even if his best had been to deposit the money at the bank. 'I was afraid,' he says (v. 25). The difference lay in the *quality of his inner relationship with his absent Lord.*

It lies in our hands to choose whether we will live in a relationship of love with Christ the Lord, or a relationship of suspicion and fear. And the sobering message is that God respects our choice: he will not – perhaps *cannot* – force us finally to change our minds, if we decide to ignore him and neglect his commission.

Application

Paul likes to think in military terms about the Christian's life. In 1 Thessalonians 5:8 he invites us to put on 'the breastplate of faith and love, and for a helmet the hope of salvation'. Here we meet his favourite trio of faith, hope and love, but ordered so as to balance present and future. 'Faith and love' are to be our breastplate – that with which we enter the battle of everyday life. And 'hope' is a 'helmet of salvation' for us: remarkably, we are soldiers confident of safety (=salvation) in the battle – and how many soldiers face battle confident of safety? Those who receive this armour from Christ (see Ephesians 6:10–20) can be absolutely confident of safety both now and on the day of judgement.

A personal audit is appropriate today! How much are faith and love the guiding principles of our everyday life? And how much is our outlook on the future marked by hope?

Christic the King – the Sunday next before Advent

Sunday between 20 and 26 November

Ezekiel 34:11–16, 20–24; Psalm 95:1–7a; Ephesians 1:15–23;
Matthew 25:31–46

The Church's year, with its rhythm of celebration covering the whole story of God's plan for the world in Christ, reaches a fitting climax on this last Sunday with a celebration of the Kingship of Christ. The whole message of the New Testament lies in the words of Ephesians 1:19–23: that God raised Christ from the dead, and has given him a position of supreme authority in the universe, commissioned to rule over all things for the Church, which is his body.

Theology

There is an inescapable exclusivism about Matthew 25 and some of the passages related to it over these weeks devoted to the reign and kingship of Christ. The spirit of our age encourages us to believe that our religion is one among many, and so cannot make exclusive claims for itself. A pluralistic world calls for a pluralistic outlook, and for glad acceptance of the equal validity of all the various human ways of grasping and conceiving God and our duty towards him.

Yes, of course. We must surely say that all religions have equal 'validity' in the sense that, as rich expressions of human culture and tradition, they have a right to continue to enrich life on earth as best they can. As we practise our religion – that colourful kaleidoscope of ecclesiastical polity, liturgy and theology that goes to make up the Christian Church and its varied life – then we certainly need to remind ourselves that there are other great religions, all practised with as much zeal and complexity as ours.

The Ephesian Christians must have found that as hard to believe as we do. They lived in a deeply pagan city, dominated by the mighty Temple of Artemis, one of the seven 'wonders' of the ancient world. The worship of Artemis was closely linked to magic and occult arts, and so they knew what Paul had in mind when he wrote of 'rule and authority and power and dominion, and every name that can be named'. Magic was all about using the power of names to gain influence, and they knew that magic worked. Could they really believe that Jesus had been raised to supreme authority as Head over all these 'powers' and 'names', and that he was ruling them 'for' his body, the Church?

We look out on a world dominated by many 'powers': not just occult, but political, military, religious, economic, social. Every day we hear of the victims of these powers. The innocent poor get caught in the cross-fire, children are exploited for adult lust, Christians are persecuted by Islamic extremists, famine takes a terrible toll because

But Karl Barth has taught us that we must distinguish fundamentally between religion and truth. The person of Jesus Christ stands in judgement over all religion, including 'Christianity'. We cannot claim rightly to have grasped him, nor to have 'contained' him in our version of the religious life, so that all must come and meet him as we do. One day all the nations will stand before his throne, and be judged by him. And the 'righteous' will be precisely those who did not tie him into their box, and claim that their religion was 'right', but those who were willing to reach out and find him among the poor of the world, even when they could not see how he could be present there. In the *favellas* and prisons of this world, in its refugee camps and hospitals and war zones, the Son of Man identifies himself with his 'brothers and sisters' who often live in complete ignorance of his presence and love . . . until one of his followers comes in his name. By such truth will the Son of Man be known, and by such truth will he judge the world.

governments have misused aid and bought arms, teenagers' desires are inflamed by unscrupulous advertising and by peer-pressure ... everywhere we see people trapped by powers beyond their control. How can we say that Christ rules over them all?

We *say it by faith*. We do not yet *see* his rule, but we *say* it. We confess it in the Creed, and take it on our lips in worship. And what is more, we *sow* his rule, because we ourselves have experienced his liberating power, and he calls us to be agents of freedom, quietly, to those around us. We are the outpost of his Kingdom, a spearhead of freedom thrust deep into enemy territory, bringing new life and light, mercy and hope.

Until his rule is finally revealed! The Gospel reading holds together so beautifully the two sides of this coin. On the one hand, there is his present, quiet rule through us, his followers, who bring touches of his love by clothing the naked, feeding the poor, visiting the prisoners and caring for the sick. He is present, all right – suffering with the victims. But on the other hand, there is his glorious future rule, when

---

Text

The beautiful parable of the sheep and goats supplements the parable of the talents, which precedes it, by unpacking the actual task of the servants. What did they do, to multiply their Lord's capital? The harsh and unpredictable master of 25:24 turns out to be a master of surprises. He was not absent at all – and they were serving him directly by using his capital to reach out to the poor.

A discussion runs as to whether 'the Son of Man' identifies himself with his poor 'brothers' (25:40), meaning his disciples, or whether he calls 'brothers' all who are poor, irrespective of whether they are disciples or not. In the first case the parable commends care within the Church; in the second case it sees Christ as already present outside the Church, and so encourages practical care as a form of outreach in his name. The second interpretation is more likely to be correct. It has the benefit of being more dramatic, more surprising (which itself is an argument in its favour), and it fits Jesus's own practice of ministering healing and preaching to all, whether disciples or not.

---

he will appear in final judgement to cleanse and redeem his world, to banish those who acquiesced in the sufferings of others, and to welcome into their inheritance those who expressed love on his behalf while the world was still astray.

Something to celebrate, indeed!

Table of First Sunday after Trinity dates and Propers

YEAR	SUNDAY CYCLE	FIRST SUNDAY AFTER TRINITY	PROPER
2002	A	2 June	4
2003	B	22 June	7
2004	C	13 June	6
2005	A	29 May	4
2006	B	18 June	6
2007	C	10 June	5
2008	A	25 May	(3)*
2009	B	14 June	6
2010	C	6 June	5
2011	A	26 June	8
2012	B	10 June	5
2013	C	2 June	4
2014	A	22 June	7
2015	B	7 June	5
2016	C	29 May	4
2017	A	18 June	6
2018	B	3 June	4
2019	C	23 June	7
2020	A	14 June	6

* For Proper 3 use Second Sunday before Lent, Option B (8th Sunday after Epiphany)

Subject index

Biblical references